From Fear to Faith

Merlin R. Carothers

Additional titles by
Merlin R. Carothers

Prison to Praise
Power in Praise
Answers to Praise
Praise Works!
Walking and Leaping
Bringing Heaven Into Hell
Victory on Praise Mountain
More Power to You
What's on Your Mind?
Let Me Entertain You
You Can Be Happy Now
Secret Sins

Published in Escondido, CA
www.merlincarothers.com
Copyright © 1997 by Merlin R. Carothers
ISBN 978-0-943026-35-0
Printed in the United States of America

Dedication

My special appreciation to my dear wife, Mary, who has edited, advised and supported me in this book, and in everything I do. Her skill and spiritual wisdom have caused my work to be far better than I could have ever done alone.

Contents

Chapter 1

The Specter of Fear

Fear lurks in the silent darkness, unwanted – hated. It's power is so great that even when ignored or denied it can still control our destiny.

My first parachute jump was a lesson in sheer terror. The Airborne instructors had vigorously indoctrinated me to believe that I was a tough paratrooper, impervious to fear. Yet I was still afraid.

Ralph Waldo Emerson wrote, "Do the thing you fear and the death of fear is certain." This adage is often true, but I was afraid during my second jump too. I didn't know it then, but my hard lessons in living and coping with the more insidious aspects of fear had just begun. I still had much to learn about fear's enormous capacity to influence our behavior.

We arrived at Fort Benning, Georgia in 1943, two hundred robust, cocky young men from all over the United States. The rigors of infantry basic training were behind us; now we were ready to confront a new challenge – Airborne training.

The grueling physical training we had endured prior to coming to Jump School had, we thought, separated the men from the boys. We were the elite of the Army, we boasted. We could do *anything*! We eagerly awaited our chance to show the Army what *real* men were.

Were we afraid? No way! We were embarking on a new and exciting adventure.

The sergeants who greeted us at the bus terminal

were seasoned Airborne veterans. They had once been greenhorns like us; they knew our attitudes. The process of ego pulverization was fierce and immediate as they rushed upon us like voracious sharks attacking minnows:

"Pick up those bags, you chicken-livered mama's boys, and let's go!"

Mama's boys? Sergeant, you don't know who you're talking to. We aren't afraid of you or anyone else!

How wrong we were.

The sergeants had one primary objective—to separate the men from the boys. In their less-than-humble opinion, the men were those who would never give up despite of injury, suffering – even torture.

In infantry basic training we had learned to run, or so we thought. But at Airborne School we never just went for a run. All we ever did was run, run, and run some more. Anytime we moved it was on the run. We ran to the latrine. We ran to chow. We ran to training sites – five, ten, or more miles. Finally we reached such a high level of fitness that we could run for hours on end without tiring. Failing meant, heaven forbid, washing out of the glorious Airborne.

But running was fun compared with the rigors at the training sites. At one site we were suspended from harnesses like those that would connect us to a parachute from which we would descend from plane to ground. The harness straps, holding our dead weight and digging into our groins, felt like thin wires straining under two hundred pounds of agonized flesh.

We hung in those harnesses while the sergeants explained, at length, the fine art of being a "famous paratrooper."

"Do you hurt, mama's boys? Want to quit?"

"Quit? No way!"

The worst thing that could happen to a sergeant

was for one of his mamas' boys to freeze in the airplane door — refuse to leap into space. His plan was to weed out any trainee who had the potential to quit, and the earlier the better. We trainees were convinced that the sergeants got a bonus for every one of us they could make a washout. None of us wanted to quit, but the sergeants, it seemed, had stronger wills. After the first grueling week our group of 200 had decreased to 150.

Before each disgraced washout departed we were lined up by the truck that would transport him to some unknown, abominable site for a truly awful assignment. The sergeants themselves led us in jeering the miserable failure. This harsh tactic was used to make those of us who remained that much more determined not to be quitters, and never to be afraid.

At the end of the second week 125 of us remained. We ended preliminary training acutely aware that the lowest level to which we could ever sink was to be a washout. So far, so good. We were fearless; we were the aristocracy of the elite. At least that's what we wanted to believe. On the morning of our first parachute jump, our barracks echoed with jubilant shouts of "Geronimo!"

The worst was yet to come.

We returned to our barracks in triumph that evening, brimming with gusto. We had made it! We had successfully completed our first jump. Only four more jumps and we would earn the coveted silver wings of the full-fledged paratrooper. Nothing could stop us now!

But we noticed that our number had shrunk from 125 to 120. What had happened to the others? We learned that they had been injured. One had broken his leg, but he would recover. Another had broken his back. No one had mentioned *that* possibility during our training.

The next morning we were a bit less enthusiastic about our upcoming jump. We tried to muster a show of bravado, but none of us could forget the man who had broken his back. A sergeant lined us up for another lecture: "Yesterday one of this group of stupid little boys failed to do what he was taught. He will not jump again. While preparing to land he was so scared that he looked down at the ground rather than straight ahead as you were all taught. He broke his back. If anyone else wants a broken back, do the same thing."

That evening several more of our comrades failed to return to the barracks. Fear set in. It had become clear to us that our chosen occupation wasn't all fun and games. Two men went AWOL. They couldn't face the humiliation of the "quitter's parade".

On our fourth jump, three men froze with fear at the open door of the plane, refusing to make the plunge into space. They were treated with the most disdain of all. That evening they were paraded before us and derided as *the most contemptible examples of cowards that three mothers ever brought into the world.* The rest of us vowed that we would never permit ourselves to be so vilified.

On the morning of our fifth jump there was an oppressive silence in our barracks. If anyone had asked, "Are you afraid?" we would have shot back, "Afraid? No!" And we would have been sincere. Each of us reasoned, "I haven't quit. Therefore, I'm not afraid." It was the quitters who had been afraid. However, if an animal with a keen sense of smell had been nearby, it would easily have detected the fear that we so stubbornly denied.

I made it through the five qualifying jumps without a scratch. Had I been afraid? Yes indeed! But I had learned to deny my fear, and finally I stood triumphantly with my comrades as our commanding general pinned the silver wings on my chest. I was now a member of the Army's most elite society of warriors. There was no reason to be afraid now. That is, not until my next leap into space.

More Lessons to Learn

My lessons in the awesome power of fear had not ended. There was more, much more, to learn. We were told of openings in various specialist schools. Communications School? At nineteen that seemed too dull. Demolitions School? Now *that* sounded exciting! So this misguided private volunteered for that risky endeavor.

There I encountered an entirely different kind of fear. The training sergeants described in explicit detail what the various explosives could do to the human body. They wanted us to be afraid, but then instructed us to control our fear rather than let it control us. A demolitions expert could not perform the required delicate work if his hands shook with fear. Several men's hands trembled as they tried to arm bombs set to explode. They were immediately disqualified.

My paratrooper training had convinced me that I was a man of steel. Now I had to prove that I had nerves of steel. I stood alone on a training field holding several pounds of plastic explosives. The sergeant asked me to demonstrate the skills we had learned. If I failed, there would be no graduation ceremony for me!

After Demolitions School, and the disastrous detours described in my first book, *Prison to Praise*, I was assigned to combat duty as an infantry soldier with the 82nd Airborne Division. My next seven parachute jumps were over Europe, where I had many opportunities to practice denying and controlling my fears. During my time in combat I wished many times that "demolitions expert" was not on my record. At times my hands shook with fear, despite my telling myself that I alone determined if and when the explosives ignited. I learned the extent to which fear can dominate everything we do.

Battle of the Bulge

The sergeant looked at me and repeated his order: "You are to take the point position tonight. Keep your eyes and ears open. Panzers are heading our way."

My heart sank as I realized that I would be alone in a foxhole. I felt like I was out in front of the entire U.S. Army. Fear began to clutch at me. I knew that if the German tanks attacked that night, there would be nothing between their dreaded panzers and me. I'd be the first Allied soldier they would run into – or over.

It was late December 1944. The Allies were bloodied and reeling from the fierce counteroffensive the Germans had launched through the Ardennes Forest of Belgium. This momentous struggle would be known to history as the Battle of the Bulge.

Outgunned and overwhelmed, my division had been forced several times to pull back. Mere foot soldiers were no match for charging tanks. According to a U.S. Army statistical report released in 1953, 19,246 American men were killed in action, suffered grievous wounds, or died while being held prisoner in that one Ardennes campaign. More than 62,000 men received nonfatal wounds, making this the heaviest single battle toll in U.S. history. British Prime Minister Winston Churchill called it the greatest American battle of the war.

The Germans used their tanks to deadly advantage, and they seemed to have an endless supply of them. Those they sent to destroy us were the biggest and best they had.

As I headed out beyond the front line of U.S. infantry, I had ample reason to be afraid. The knowledge that other Americans would be in foxholes behind me was no comfort. I would have been immensely reassured had I seen a battalion of American tanks racing to my rescue.

I was in A Company, 508th Airborne Infantry Regiment, 82ndAirborne, one of the Army's most elite divisions. We felt that we were the best of the best. But I wasn't feeling particularly brave as I continued forward.

I dug in at my designated position, the foxhole my only protection. No sergeant had to order "dig deeper, soldier." I carried my trusty M1 rifle and a few antitank grenades that I lined up before me. My rifle would shoot straight, but the grenades seldom landed where one aimed them.

As night fell I waited in my foxhole for I knew not what. I was really afraid.

Why did the sergeant choose me for point position? "Point position" is military jargon for sending a soldier out in front of the rest of his unit as it advances through hostile territory. He acts as a scout and "trip wire". In the event of ambush or land mines, he is the unlucky one. Who wants to be point man? Nobody! Aside from sounding an alarm, what could I be expected to do in a panzer attack? I didn't feel capable of turning back even one tank, let alone hundreds. I was on guard duty, required to be alert to any signs of attack. I had no illusions about becoming a hero. My primary desire was merely to survive the war in one piece.

As I listened to the wind rustling through the trees,

I thought I heard the approach of panzers. I shook my head and tried to think of something else. I tried to enjoy the moonlight glistening off the snow, but that lasted only a short while. Then I imagined that German soldiers were crawling silently toward me. The glistening I saw was probably from piano wire that would be used to strangle me. I shuddered.

The rest of the night was more of the same. My fear of the panzers haunted me, though I tried to keep it at bay. I was practicing the fine art of being afraid.

An old army saying goes: "There are no atheists in foxholes." That was certainly true for me that night. Except for a brief time in my youth, I hadn't had much use for God. But in the cold and darkness of my foxhole, I cried out to Him to help me not to be afraid.

Seeing an enemy tank charging right at you is an awesome experience. Talk about fear! *That's* the time to be afraid!

But seeing a friendly tank, out in front of you with its guns pointed at the enemy, is an entirely different experience. That tank is working *for* you – for your good.

When you liken your difficulties to a deadly enemy tank, you will be afraid. That's when you need a totally new perspective.

God can cause our problems to work for us. If we trust Him, He will turn them around, facing the enemy, and make them work for our good. Once we see that picture clearly and believe that God is working, we will have the joy of seeing Him accomplish many good things in us. As we trust God to work for our good, He will eventually release incredible joy within us.

Finally morning dawned. The dreaded panzers had not come! I had survived being on point. In the haze I saw twelve of our soldiers move off to my right. They were advancing! I was less afraid then and I thought,

Great, now there will be someone else between those panzers and me! Then I saw an entire company of American soldiers right behind the first group. As some 150 men moved forward, my mind and muscles relaxed for the first time in many hours.

Then I saw a sight that *really* warmed my heart. A column of our Sherman tanks was moving toward the front, perhaps a part of General Patton's "Blood and Guts" Third Army. Patton was a formidable fighter, one of our heroes. If his army was involved, I thought we might get out alive. The clanking and rumbling of those tanks were music to my ears.

The Battle of the Bulge was fought many years ago. When I look back at that dramatic episode in my life, I marvel at how effectively God used it to teach me some very important lessons. While fighting in the Battle of the Bulge, I was also engaged in a personal battle: would I be controlled by fear or by faith? I began to see that both faith and fear are common in life, but that they are powerful enemies and opposing spiritual forces. I discovered that it is a spiritual law that fear breeds lack of confidence which, in turn, produces defeat. Yet it is an equal and opposite spiritual law that faith breeds confidence and – victory!

Fear is like a horde of enemy tanks that threatens us and makes us cower. Faith is like an army of friendly tanks that protects and allows us to advance victoriously. In this light, have you ever felt as if a hostile army was out there waiting for a chance to squash you, to annihilate you? If you have, I know exactly how you feel.

Chaplain Carothers

I returned to the Army as a chaplain in 1953, with good reasons to be no longer afraid. I believed and clung to the promise of 1 John 4:18 that, *perfect love casts out fear*. But I was still very much afraid to jump out of a perfectly good airplane while far above the earth.

As a chaplain in the Airborne, I made 78 additional jumps. Paratroopers who carefully followed instructions usually broke no bones, although we always hit the ground with a jolt. I went to the hospital many times after jumps, to visit men who had been injured. Only a few of them were seriously hurt, but their injuries grieved me deeply. Such injuries did little to alleviate my battle with fear.

The injuries I sustained didn't quiet my fears either. Part of me believed that paratroopers were protected by hosts of angels whose primary duty was to ensure that we lived to jump another day. The first inkling that my guardian angel might be off duty was when I made a two-point landing – feet first, then on my head. I managed to roll up my chute, carry it off the field, and sit down under a tree. I sat there for two hours before I realized where I was and that I had made another jump.

On two other occasions I was knocked unconscious upon impact with the ground. Other wayward landings in trees, ditches, water, and on rocks convinced me that parachuting could be exceedingly dangerous.

Night jumps were the worst of all, holding gut-gripping terror for those of us who were halfway sane. We sat nervously in bucket seats until the jumpmaster yelled, "Stand up!" Our static lines were hooked behind us, denying us the security of seeing ourselves attached to something solid. Interior lights were turned off so our eyes could adapt to the outside blackness.

To the right of the exit doors was a red light about the size of a quarter. It looked forebodingly evil, yet every eye was drawn to it. When it went out, a green one flashed on. It meant, "go!" Not "go if you feel like it." Not "go if you aren't afraid." It meant "swallow your terror and leap forth into the dark void." Will my chute open? Every paratrooper wondered.

Then came the terrifying plunge into black space, the air shrieking past our ears as we descended into the bottomless pit of darkness. For seconds that seemed endless we were gripped in a fist of pure force as the prop-blast flung us like cannonballs into the night. We tumbled swiftly through blackness until finally we reached the end of the unyielding static line attached to the plane. Wham! One instant we were plummeting downward, the next we were reversed upward with an abrupt and violent jerk.

Once the chute opened there was the odd sensation of floating utterly alone in space. We knew we were falling, though, and we steeled ourselves to meet Earth's crushing embrace.

If we could see the ground before landing, we could soften our impact with a sudden strong pull on the four risers, releasing them just before we met the earth. The air, momentarily trapped in the chute, would then soften our landing. With the old World War II-chutes, however, the sensation was more like jumping from a car at thirty miles an hour. Actually, the approaching earth was not the greatest fear; it gives a little. It was the rocks, trees, or buildings that could break our bones – or worse.

Why would any sane person face such dangers if it were not absolutely necessary? Men seem to have a desire to prove their bravery, and I was no exception. I continued to jump, despite the ever-present fear during my ninety leaps into infinity. I am grateful for the valuable lessons on how to cope – and how not to cope – with fear.

As a paratrooper I learned to deal with fear by

denying it, hoping it would go away. I tried to hide my emotions, telling myself and others that I wasn't afraid. My self-deception didn't help much, however, as long as I was really afraid.

As a demolitions expert I learned that fear was not to be denied, but controlled. My survival and that of my comrades often depended on my ability to act as though I was not afraid, even while in the grip of terror. This struggle cost me all the energy and willpower I could muster. My mind and spirit were being permeated by fear that threatened to control me.

As a chaplain I knew that God's influence was much more powerful than the apprehension I fought when I jumped from a plane. Still, fear darkened my spirit and clutched at my guts, mocking my faith. Why couldn't I shake it? I returned from all jumps emotionally exhausted from the inward battles. Fighting the constant fear drained me.

You may be living in a situation that often brings fear into your heart, and you may be doing your best to persevere. Yet fear and frustration persist. Since my parachute-jumping days, I have learned things I wish I'd known long ago.

Learning to Defeat Fear

My journey of discovery began as I learned to praise and thank God for all the circumstances in my life, the difficult as well as the good. As I thanked Him for the things I feared most, an amazing thing began to happen: the fears subsided. Slowly it dawned on me that there *is* a way to conquer fear, and that we can learn how to be delivered from its insidious power. I had taken the first step when I began to thank God *for* my fear rather than in spite of it. As long as I fought fear by denying or controlling it, I was in its power. When

I admitted being afraid and thanked God for my circumstances and my own helplessness, the opposite of what I expected happened. Instead of being engulfed by terror, the power of fear was broken, and the things I feared were much less formidable.

It is a curious paradox that as long as we fight fear, it remains our tormentor. But when we meet it with gratitude and faith, it is defeated and, in fact, becomes our ally.

It's been a sometimes painful but wonderfully exciting journey to work toward freedom from fear.

FROM FEAR TO FAITH

Chapter 2

Controlled by Fear - Or by Faith?

We live by fear or by faith, and the one we choose makes all the difference in the world.

God has provided me with abundant training in what it's like to be afraid. At the time I did not appreciate His methods, but now I see His careful attention to the details I needed to understand. I have learned that life is like a school; we must graduate from one grade in order to advance to the next. So I am describing a few of the classes I was required to attend.

Walking through minefields during World War II really got my attention. I learned that fear could cause me to perspire even in freezing temperatures! On one occasion as we inched through the Black Forest in Germany at about one step per minute, we perspired so much that our clothing became soaking wet. In our training we had been told how dangerous minefields were, but our reaction usually was, I hear what you are saying, but it's not relevant – that will never happen to me.

But the horror of seeing other men blown apart by mines gave me ample reason to be terrified. Every time I put a foot on the ground I thought it might be my last step. At the time I had no understanding of how to have faith that God would take care of me. I did not realize that He wants to daily guide our steps.

You are not likely to walk through military-style minefields, but similar challenges may lie ahead of you. I pray that your journey toward faith will be an exciting pilgrimage into ever-higher levels of faith.

A healthy, natural fear alerts us to danger, and helps us live in our corrupted world. But when fear is exaggerated or misdirected, we suffer. We are robbed of faith, joy, strength, and possibly even life itself. The Bible tells us 365 times not to be afraid. God wants to encourage us to be fearless. He also wants us to know how dangerous and destructive fear can be.

Consider the human body. Reasonable fear protects us from foolishly putting ourselves at risk. But too much fear can destroy the body. It can make the heart race, our blood pressure rise and can cause other internal reactions that are harmful to us. That is simply the way God designed us.

Medical science reveals that if we spend years worrying that we may someday get a certain disease, the fear itself could eventually create it. If we are ill, fear may even prevent us from getting well.

We are not helpless victims of the things we fear most: misfortune, pain, poverty, loneliness, ridicule, failure – even death. Some of these things will indeed happen, but the Scriptures tell us not to fear them. Fear may try to stalk us, but faith can conquer it. God did not design us to be dominated by fear. And we have the power to *choose* to live by the power of faith.

Fear mocks, "Yesterday was bad, today is horrible, and tomorrow will be even worse. And you can't do anything about it."

But in faith, each of us can declare, "God was with me yesterday. He is with me today, and He will be with me forever. I can do all things through Christ who gives me strength. Because of Him I live."

Fear wants us to retreat and shrink back because we think our efforts will lead only to failure.

Faith encourages us to advance. It causes us to believe that we can succeed. Then we can move boldly forward from triumph to triumph.

Fear wants us to turn away from spiritual battle until eventually we forget that a battle is being waged!

Faith inspires us to be bold for God.

Fear is an opiate. It drugs us into thinking that we don't have to do what God would have us do. It makes us relax in our easy chairs and expect someone else to do what we should be doing. Fear can make us indifferent, apathetic, and even cowardly.

Faith gives us the confidence to do what needs to be done. Faith motivates and strengthens us. It stimulates, challenges, and gives us courage to persevere and overcome.

Fear can affect the way we feel; it can also contribute to the way we look and act. When fear controls us we may look tense, angry, or depressed. When fear controls us our troubles and trials seem too much to bear. Our shoulders are slumped. We feel terrible, and we show it. Or we clench our teeth behind a mask of forced cheer, denying to ourselves and to others that fear exists.

In contrast, faith causes us to pull our shoulders back. Our steps become lighter, and whatever our troubles, they become a hundred times easier to bear. Believing that God loves us and works in everything that happens to us for our good, causes our hearts and minds to work better. High blood pressure decreases. Tense nerves relax. Attitudes change, and we smile more. Faith enables us to be joyful whatever our circumstances may be.

Joyous believing can cause us to:
- be more successful.
- have new friends.
- have a better marriage.
- overcome feelings of inferiority.
- conquer bitterness and anger.

- overcome needless feelings of guilt.

The benefits of joyful believing are endless. The Bible declares, *Be strong in the Lord and in the power of His might* (Eph. 6:10).

If we choose to be weak, Satan can destroy everything of value to us, so I propose that we learn to be strong "in the power of His might!" We must learn how to have the kind of faith that will give us freedom from fear, bring answers to our prayers, and change us.

I promise that as you are released from fear, you will experience new pleasure in every hour of every day, new peace of mind, and new excitement over the challenges and achievements of your life.

Chapter 3

Authority Over Fear

The apostle Paul was not afraid of deadly scorpions. His lack of fear caused people who had never heard about Jesus to become interested in everything he had to say. Paul was convinced that animals, even poisonous ones, could not harm him (Acts 28:3–6). However, when I was taking the Jungle Expert Course in Panama, I did not understand that I had any authority over fear.

We were trudging through a dense tangle of vines and tropical shrubs that completely obliterated the sky. There was no path, so we used machetes to hack our way through the undergrowth. Then it happened – so quickly that I didn't have even a second to prepare. A twelve-foot snake dropped from the trees, its eyes staring right into my face! I had never seen a snake longer than three feet, and my heart immediately recognized that it lived in a body that was terrified. It seems strange now, but I was too frightened to make a sound, or even to move. The snake looked me in the eye, decided it didn't want me for lunch, dropped to the ground and slithered on its way.

While I was enduring the jungle training and other similar schooling, I had no idea that God would use these experiences to prepare me for two unexpected events:

1. My deployment to Vietnam, where both the temperature and humidity hovered at a sweltering 97 degrees.

2. Being selected to be promoted from major to

lieutenant colonel on the Army's 5 percent list.

The Army is permitted by Congress to promote a maximum of 5 percent of its officers who do not have sufficient time-in-grade to be considered. Getting promoted is an important event in an officer's life. Many officers spend thirty years dreaming of making the coveted 5 percent list, but it never occurred to me that I would ever be considered. To my knowledge, no chaplain had ever been on the list, so I assumed that we were excluded from consideration.

When my name appeared on the list, it seemed to me that God must have written it in when no one was looking. Perhaps, however, the rigorous training had something to do with it.

I mention these experiences to illustrate that God will go to any length to prepare us for our next assignment. Some experiences are difficult, while others are delightful. God knows the correct balance necessary to prepare His servants for their best use.

In so many unconventional ways, God has helped me to understand how faith can overcome our fears. The things I have learned have not given me any quick, easy solutions, but God has convinced me that fear of *any* kind can be eliminated by faith.

The Smell of Fear

A dog knows when a person is afraid of him. He smells the distinct aroma of fear.

As pastor of a church in Escondido, California, I preached a sermon on taking authority over our fears, and I used an illustration of how to confront an aggressive dog. The very next day a member had a chance to practice what he had learned. His neighbor had left a water hose turned on, and water was flooding both their yards. Efforts to alert the people next door failed, so Jim climbed the fence between the yards. He turned the water off and was heading back when he heard a scurrying noise and an angry snarl. The neighbor's newly acquired Doberman Pinscher, fangs bared, was charging toward him.

Jim froze, then remembered my sermon. He stepped toward the dog, pointed his finger, and shouted, "Down!" The dog obeyed.

Keeping an eye on the dog, Jim again started toward the fence. When the Doberman saw him retreat, it leaped up and charged again. Jim again forcefully commanded, "Down!" and once again the animal obeyed. By that time Jim had made it to the top of the fence before the dog dashed toward him. The racket alerted the neighbor's wife, who came running from the house. From his perch on the fence, my friend told her what had occurred.

She exclaimed, "Oh, my gosh! He's a trained guard dog and has bitten several people!" My friend, although shaken, was thankful that he had learned one benefit of taking authority over fear.

We who believe and trust in God have the ability to examine the source of our fears and combat them. We can use the tools that God has given us.

In my paratrooper days I tried in vain to take authority over my fears by denying, controlling, or fighting them. I may have seemed to be in charge of them, but they were always there to haunt me. Though I tried to insist that I wasn't afraid, I didn't even believe it myself. My fears did not go away, no matter how forcefully I sought to take control.

A trained dog will not respond to a command from someone who doubts his own authority to give it. Dog trainers must train owners as well. My friend who commanded his neighbor's dog to lie down had become convinced by my words the day before that the dog would accept his authority.

So, in taking authority over our fears, we must have faith that God has given us authority over them. We are told in James 4:7 to *submit to God. Resist the devil and he will flee from you.*

We are not told to close our eyes and pretend that there is no devil. Or no snarling dog. Or no fear. The dog was real. It would be only natural to be afraid. But when we understand something about the nature of dogs, and the authority we can have over them, we are able to use that knowledge. In Christ we have been given authority over our fears. Knowing something about the nature of our fears, and our God-given authority over them, frees us to use that power.

Some fears turn out to be completely unfounded, even imaginary. Once we know the facts, our fear dissipates. It is like turning on the light in a room that once held the terror of darkness.

Such was my inordinate teenage fear of girls. Throughout high school I often saw young ladies I wanted to date. I would walk toward one I saw as especially attractive, then turn away at the last minute. I never thought of being afraid on the football field, but a romantic approach toward a girl caused me tongue-tied terror. Even in my first year of college my tongue failed me when I tried to express interest in a female classmate.

Once a friend arranged for me to escort a winsome coed to a banquet. Actually, she was beautiful, seen by many as the most sought-after girl on campus. She was sixteen and I seventeen. I was nervous.

I arrived at the women's dormitory to pick up my date, pacing the floor as I waited. Then, there she was gliding toward me, smiling and graceful in her dazzling evening gown. I fumbled with my tie. My face grew warm. I was speechless, and had to remind myself to breathe. I managed a smile and awkward greeting; then, curiously light-headed, I escorted my first beauty queen to the banquet.

Throughout that evening I rehearsed over and over how I would invite her to go out with me again, but when I opened my mouth, my tongue seemed paralyzed. I went off to war at the end of the school year and never again got the opportunity to ask my campus queen for a date. Later I learned that she had been interested in me for what she saw as my intense spiritual zeal. How foolish I had been to allow fear to control my actions! My fears were utterly imaginary, carrying no real threats.

I remember when my shyness toward girls left me. I was walking down Main Street in Beaver Falls, Pennsylvania, with Grandfather Carothers. I was on my first leave after graduation from Airborne School. At nineteen I was ready to face the world. Three young ladies spied my gleaming parachute boots, jump wings, and uniform. They ran up, and all three began to hug me. Each told me her name and asked if she could see me that evening.

A light turned on. Girls were interested in boys! How could I have lived so long and not understood such an obvious and basic fact? From then on when I saw an attractive girl, I no longer had to wrestle with fear. It was gone. Now the new and enlightened Merlin could walk up to any member of the opposite sex and utter the important opening words: "Hello, haven't I met you somewhere?" I could have spoken those words on hundreds of past occasions, but my fear had restrained me.

Think of it this way: If we tried to walk on a two-by-four board as a bridge between two twenty-five-story buildings, most of us would be terrified. Why? Because we can't walk on a two-by-four board? It depends on where the board is. If we placed it on the ground, we wouldn't be afraid to walk on it. The same board, the same person, but no fear. Many of us seem to believe that the "board" we fear spans a bottomless chasm when, in fact, it rests firmly and safely on the ground.

It is just as pointless to say, "I'm not afraid," if indeed you are, as it is to say, "I believe," if you don't. The objective is to be delivered from the power of fear and to clearly and honestly believe what you say you believe.

Freedom from fear begins with one step: admitting that we are afraid. Reasonable fear is an ally once we recognize it and place it in proper perspective. Our reluctance to admit fear can make us deny, fight, or try to control it. But in doing so it then controls us, even to the point of paralyzing or killing us.

Solo Flying

I'll never forget my first solo flight in an airplane. Since my early teens I had dreamed that someday I would be a pilot, but it wasn't until I was twenty-nine that I fulfilled my dream. I owned only half interest in the plane, and the little Cessna had barely enough power to take off, but to me it was a mighty worker of miracles. It thrust me and my instructor up, up into the wild blue yonder. I was ecstatic. My dream had become a reality.

Every flight was packed with excitement. Everything the instructor asked me to do gave me pure joy. Heading back to the airport always made me unhappy. I yearned to fly into space and orbit the world.

During every minute of my training flights, I looked forward to the moment when the instructor would say, "Today you will make your solo flight." That was the ultimate, the very summit, of success – to fly all by myself! Each day I determined to handle my beautiful flying machine so expertly that the instructor would see that I was ready.

The moment of supreme ecstasy finally arrived. I had completed a successful landing when the instructor said, "Stop the plane, let me out, and take off on your own."

As I taxied down the runway I shouted, "This is it!"

Then, the glorious moment. I was at the beginning of the runway. I was ready to go. With no control tower on that little country airfield, the time of takeoff was up to me.

After a few deep breaths I gripped the little throttle and carefully pushed it full forward. The "mighty" engine burst into action, and I began to roll down the runway. After about two hundred feet the plane began pulling to the left, although the runway went straight ahead. I quickly turned the steering wheel to the right, but the plane kept going left. What was wrong?

Then I saw disaster in the making directly ahead — six men were digging a ditch on the left edge of the runway. My plane was racing straight toward them. In panic I wrenched the wheel more to the right but the plane would not respond. With a seemingly obstinate determination the little propeller kept pulling me rapidly toward the workers who were oblivious to my approach.

My desperation mounted. The next few seconds seemed like forever. The whirling propeller could kill the workers. The frail craft could explode and ignite the gasoline. Seven lives were in peril!

The left wheel veered off the runway; the point of no return had arrived. Everything the instructor had said vanished from my mind. Fear took over. With the propeller now only a few yards from the workers, I managed a mighty heave on the controls. The plane lifted a few feet off the ground, missed the men and a fence by inches, and finally rose into the sky. I was safe, but my pride was shattered. Fear had utterly destroyed my opportunity for a splendid performance.

With instructions only to circle the field and land, I dreaded facing the instructor. This student was a miserable failure.

"Well, Carothers, what did you do wrong?"

"Everything!"

"Do you know exactly what you did?" Yes, I knew. The instructor had warned me dozens of times that the steering wheel does not control the direction of an airplane on the ground.

"You turn a car with the steering wheel. You turn an airplane with rudders. Use your feet. Push the left rudder for left and the right rudder for right." In our dual takeoffs I had pushed the right rudder for a straight direction on the runway. When I was alone, however, fear had taken over, and everything I knew about controlling a plane on the ground had flown out the window.

Instead of chewing me out, the instructor went over what I had done wrong, and why, saying that panic was common on a first solo, and that my reaction was not unusual. He had me take off a dozen more times with him. Finally he said, "Now you're on your own again." I made a perfect takeoff, and soon I became a licensed pilot. Since then I have flown for many hours and been in tight situations, but never again did I freeze in panic like I did on that first harrowing solo flight.

Flying helped me to put fear into proper perspective. Instead of controlling me, fear became my ally. The guard dog of fear keeps me on my toes, and reminds me of my limitations. Most of all it reminds me of my need to depend on God. It compels me to maintain my flying skills or stay out of the pilot's seat. It warns me that panic can turn fear into a snarling attacker, threatening to kill. But when we take authority over it, and calmly say, "Down!" as with a charging dog, it frees our minds for the tasks ahead.

We can make an ally out of reasonable fear. In the following chapters we will examine some common roots of unreasonable fear. First, however, we will look at the source that conquers fear — our joyous faith!

Chapter 4

Faith to Climb Mountains

My wife Mary and I loaded our motorhome for an impromptu visit to Yosemite National Park. What a magnificent sight it was!

There I learned a lesson that would bring about important changes in my attitude about many things. This process began on our second day there.

Five people stood near our campsite, peering up at Washington Tower. What are they studying so intently? I wondered. They passed a pair of binoculars from one to the other. Obviously something intrigued them.

As I studied the smooth, solid stone that seemed to jut straight up for twenty-five hundred feet, I could see nothing but rock. We were about three hundred yards from the base of the gigantic, awesome tower that reaches toward the sky. One of the group said, "Look, he's moving upward!" I looked, but there was no "he" in sight.

We had binoculars with us, so I decided to see what had captivated those folk's attention. At first I saw nothing but the mountain. Then, about one thousand feet up the face of the tower, I saw what looked like a bright red dot. It was near two other spots, all linked by what appeared to be a rope.

I felt a knot in the pit of my stomach. Those spots were *people*! Were they crazy? Later I inquired around the campground to see if anyone knew what was going on.

"Oh, sure," said one man. "A different group of

climbers goes up there every day."

"How far up do they go?"

"All the way. Usually they make it part way in a day, spend the night on a ledge or hanging in a net, and then finish the next day."

"How many are killed?"

"Oh, they know what they're doing. They seldom even get hurt. Last year one man broke a leg, and a helicopter had to lift him off."

For a few days I avidly watched the groups of climbers. The knot in my stomach subsided a little as, through seven-power binoculars, I watched those tiny "spots" always get to the top by nightfall on their second day. But what kind of people would risk life and limb to engage in such a hazardous sport? The mountain seemed all but impossible for humans to scale.

Mary and I made our way to its base, where the climb seemed even more formidable. The surface seemed nearly as smooth as a cement highway. How could a person climb even twenty feet? I wondered. To scale the entire mountain seemed impossible.

As we walked along we came upon a group of six men. Five of them were being trained in rock climbing. The sixth man had a rope that went through a pulley fastened about one hundred feet up. One end was attached to a trainee; the instructor held the other. As the student climbed a few feet up, the instructor pulled in the slack to keep him in a steady, safe grip.

We were enthralled. The student probed about with his fingers, finally thrusting them into a nearly invisible perpendicular crack. He shifted his weight to the right, then to the left. His shoes appeared to be very thin, and the soles seemed comprised of a coarse, sand-paper–like material. Attached to the back of his belt was a pouch containing powder for his hands. The shoes seemed to cling to the smooth rock as though they had suction cups on them.

I realized then that rock climbing is a skill that can be learned. My appetite for details was whetted, so I began to read about rock climbing. I was seeking understanding, however, *not* participation.

One detail taught me a very important lesson about life. To ascend a high and precarious solid-stone mountain, a climber must learn to pace himself. This is the ability to get the most mileage, or altitude, from his available energy. If he uses up his reservoir of strength, exhaustion comes. If he climbs 2,400 feet up a 2,500-foot mountain and runs out of vitality, he may be stuck there in the dark, or in a storm. I would not want to face such problems! Making it to 2,400 feet isn't enough. He must make it to the top or to some safe spot en route.

Climbers use every conceivable means to conserve their energy. Prior to the trip, they eat foods that provide maximum nourishment. But food means weight, so they carefully select what they carry with them. Clothing at high altitudes and in chilling winds needs to be warm, but light. Ropes and all equipment need to be of minimum weight but maximum strength. Expertise is required too in the quantity and quality of the pack, sleeping bag, 150 feet of rope, hammer, webbing, carabiners, pitons, chock stones, wedges, nuts, and angle irons.

But most important, instructors insist, is the *attitude* of the climber. He must not be anxious or afraid. Why? The obvious reason is that fear inhibits the body's ability to function. A less obvious reason is the source of my important lesson.

Fear and anxiety consume too much energy. Really? Yes! Serious climbers cannot afford the luxury of anxiety. Fear causes energy to evaporate.

People who would scale challenging mountains must first learn to be so confident in themselves that they thoroughly enjoy what they are doing. Instructors say, "Of course, everyone will eventually have anxious moments. But that has to be rare. Climbing must be exhilarating and fun, or the climber will be too exhausted to reach the top."

Most of us are never pitted against tasks that use maximum energy resources, so we seldom learn what causes our energy to be lost. If we're tired, we simply stop to rest or eat. Rock climbers often can't avail themselves of such luxuries. Their lives and their success depend on reaching the top in the required time. If they run out of energy, they could make a fatal mistake – for themselves and those who depend on them.

Some Christians never persevere long enough to climb a spiritual mountain. If they fail to reach their goal quickly enough, they simply give up the task. Christians who are determined to reach certain goals need maximum spiritual energy. I have learned that this energy is quickly dissipated by fear. The Bible repeatedly cautions us against fear and anxiety. They cause our ability to reach spiritual goals to dissipate like energy seeping from a battery.

A battery-operated radio can pick up messages from a broadcasting station. But as the battery weakens and then dies, the radio can no longer receive the signals.

This analogy is far from accurate, but it helps me to understand a vital factor in my spiritual life. If I allow myself to be anxious about anything, my spiritual battery gets weaker. Then, when God has a message for me, my ability to receive His message is so weak that I can't hear what He is saying. The volume of His broadcast hasn't decreased in the slightest – only my ability to receive it.

If you wonder why you lack the spiritual energy to go out and tell others the good news of the gospel, perhaps fear has stolen your resources.

Picture Christians who have serious problems and have learned through years of practice to spend endless hours in worry. They wish they had made different decisions. They are afraid of the future. They cry out for direction from God, who speaks, but they can't hear Him. Their spiritual ability to hear is overwhelmed by their fears.

Would-be rock climbers could choose to stay on the ground, but you and I have no choice. We must be about the task of fulfilling our purpose here on earth.

We must daily surrender our self-proclaimed right to worry about our health, our job, the boss not liking us, our children, what our spouses might do, and so on. I have never heard a clear word from God or received a miracle for another person or myself unless I was abiding in His peace.

You may say, "That isn't fair. God should help me when I'm upset. That's when I need help the most." But regardless of our wishes, if we insist on our right to be anxious and fearful, we lose spiritual strength and cannot be victorious.

Yes, other people do not always understand why you are afraid. They haven't walked in your shoes. But for all of us the goal is still the same – to be free of fear.

The Bible says, *Don't be anxious* (Matt. 6:34 TLB). It's not that God doesn't like anxious people. He wants us to learn how to trust Him.

The Army taught me how to make a parachute jump. The trainers told me to relax and not to worry. Not be worried? You gotta be kidding! The chute might not open! But they emphasized, "Don't be afraid when you leave the plane, and don't be afraid when you hit the ground."

Fortunately for me, the night before our first jump I went to sleep the minute my head hit the pillow. Other men lay awake all night. The next morning as they stood at the open door of the plane, they were tense, worried, and anxious. Some were so tired that they couldn't recall what we had been taught. Their muscles were tight; they were primed for an accident. Instead of leaping boldly into the air as they had been trained to do, they fell out, and often became entangled in the dozens of lines of the parachute. Their fear and lack of confidence in what they had been taught brought them needless pain. And, at times, death!

An anxious paratrooper can be compared to the small branch of a dead tree. Consider how easy it is to snap a brittle, unbending twig, while a live branch will bend easily without breaking.

In nearly fifteen years of paratrooper training, I saw many men seriously injured because they had no faith in themselves or in their equipment. They left the plane with a tense knot of fear in their guts, and upon reaching the ground, were still so tense that they broke legs, and some, even their spines. Not one of them wanted to get hurt, but they were controlled by their fears, and had very little faith in their parachutes. This resulted in unnecessary suffering and tragedy.

God says, Don't be anxious. Don't be anxious at any time for any reason. A fearful paratrooper and a worried Christian, then, seem to have some characteristics in common.

Consider our efforts to communicate with God, and to ask His help with our problems. He knows that our anxiety separates us from the help He wants to give us. If we fail to follow His instruction to trust Him, we approach prayer with a tense, anxious spirit. Then God seems far away. If our faith is weak, our efforts to trust God can easily crumble. We may never crash into the ground like a paratrooper, but anxiety and fear can delay the normal growth and maturity of our seed of faith.

I don't know why I could sleep so peacefully the night before my first parachute jump. I don't know, either, why some people can always pray with confidence and faith that God will hear and answer them.

I do, however, know that some of my friends were seriously injured when they were anxious about jumping. I know, too, that anxiety is exactly the opposite of faith, and that many prayers go unanswered when we are anxious.

Joy That Replaces Fear

When we know why our prayers are not being answered, we can then concentrate on learning how to get rid of our fears and anxieties. Praise to God for everything can become our powerful ally.

The key is to release everything in our lives to God, and believe that He is working in and through everything for our good. We then receive and rejoice in the answer to our prayer even before God does anything. We have peace in the knowledge that He has the right solution. If this seems too simple an explanation, please remember the paratrooper.

Picture the young man floating to the ground on his first jump. The last thing he wants is pain. Not one parachutist wants to be injured. Yet the one who is most afraid is the one most likely to be hurt.

The person most afraid that his prayers won't be answered is the one most likely to have little faith and, therefore, unanswered prayers.

Most of us have said to ourselves, "I believe! I

believe!" when we really meant, "I want to believe, but my doubts are stronger than my believing."

I've learned a most helpful way to strengthen my faith. We know that this Scripture is true: *We know that all that happens to us is working for our good if we love God and are fitting into his plans* (Rom. 8:28 TLB). Because we know this is true, we can know that God is in control of every detail of our lives. When this truth is firmly settled in our hearts and minds, we find that it is not too difficult to give Him the thanks and praise that He desires in every situation in our lives (1 Thes. 5:18). As we do, we find – to our surprise – that praising and thanking God for our problems (as Eph. 5:20 tells us) actually cause our faith to grow and keep on growing.

In turn, our faith and confidence in God bring us joy: *Now when he had brought them into his house, he set food before them; and he rejoiced, having believed in God* (Acts 16:34); and *Though now you do not see Him, yet believing, you rejoice with joy inexpressible and full of glory* (1 Peter 1:8).

But Jesus cautioned us that the joy we experience when we believe will leave us if we stop believing: *The ones on the rock are those who, when they hear, receive the word with joy; and these have no root, who believe for a while and in time of temptation fall away* (Luke 8:13).

As we say, "God, I believe You are answering my prayer in the way that will bring me the most good," we receive joy. This is a natural response to believing that God has all the details of life under His control. Jesus taught us to have faith like that of a little child. When a child believes she will receive the very best, what happens? Her face lights up! So, practice smiling when you say, "God, I believe You." Faith causes joy to increase, and that makes it fun to practice believing God.

I've learned a crucial lesson: fear and faith are reflected in our faces. Mark 9:20 tells us that the demon in a boy saw Jesus. That means that demons can see us!

The Bible doesn't tell us that evil spirits can read our thoughts. But if they see joy in us, they must know it is the joy of the Lord. They then want to get away from us, just as they always wanted to get away from Jesus. Do you see how important it is for us to learn how to live in the incredible power of joy?

Even before Jesus came to earth, men prophesied that He would have *exultant joy and gladness above and beyond [His] companions* (Heb. 1:9 amplified). The Greek word for gladness, agalliasis, means "much leaping." The Living Bible says that Jesus had *more gladness . . . [than] anyone else* (Heb. 1:9).

Have you noticed that Jesus could look at people and see that they had the faith to be healed? The Bible doesn't say He used His ability to read minds; He saw something in them. He must have seen the expectant joy in their faces as they believed He was going to heal them.

When we believe something good is about to happen, we react with joy. Joy and believing work so closely together that it is sometimes difficult to separate one from the other. Joy is a dynamo that can cause our faith to work. Even the demons must know this.

I believe this is why God has given us instructions in Philippians and Ephesians to rejoice always, and to sing and make melody in our hearts. He knows that we are vulnerable to all kinds of torments if we aren't empowered with His joy.

God's joy in us is a little like gasoline is to a car

engine. Joy equals power; joy causes us to get where we want to go.

Many cry, "Give me what I need (want), and then I'll shout with the voice of triumph." But the laws of faith work the same for you and me as they did for Abraham, Isaac, David, Peter, and Paul. When we believe, we receive. Joy is the fuel that creates the power of our faith. Little joy results in:

- little strength.
- unfulfilled desires.
- no overflowing of hope.

According to 2 Corinthians 3:18, *we reflect the glory of the Lord*. The word used for glory means "dazzling" or "glittering." I strongly recommend that all of us learn to have that glory working in us.

If you walk into a dark room, you might stub your toes, bang your head, or even fall flat on your face. But find a tiny light switch, turn it on, and enjoy the light as it flows from a distant power plant. As long as the switch stays on, the power keeps flowing.

God's unlimited joy will flow into our lives if we keep the switch of praise turned on. Absence of joy causes us to stumble in the darkness of life's problems. We can't create joy, any more than a light switch can create light. But we are able to turn on God's joy by giving Him the continual sacrifice of praise (Heb. 13:15). I bumbled along for many years in gloom. I was anxious about my physical problems, grieved over deaths in my family, and I suffered anxieties about the future. The horrors I had experienced during several wars haunted my dreams. Until I learned to praise and thank God for everything in my life.

If darkness seems to surround you, don't give up. This book might be just what you need to turn on God's magnificent light switch.

Christian author Corrie ten Boom wrote about her experiences as a captive in a German concentration camp during World War II. She and her sister, Betsy, were cast into a flea-infested barracks in the worst prison camp in Poland. What darkness! Betsy told Corrie that they needed to thank God for every detail of their trials, including the fleas. At first Corrie refused to praise the Lord for the horrible little insects, but then she agreed and united with Betsy. During their months at the camp they were able to hold prayer and Bible study meetings freely, without the guards intruding. The reason? The guards would not enter that barracks because of the fleas. As a direct result of her concentration camp experiences, Corrie went on to win thousands of people to Christ.

In William Law's eighteenth-century classic, *A Serious Call to a Devout and Holy Life*, he wrote:

Would you know who is the greatest saint in the world? It is not he who prays most or fasts most; it is not he who gives most alms, or is most eminent for temperance, chastity, or justice, but it is he who is always thankful to God, who wills everything that God willeth, who receives everything as an instance of God's goodness, and has a heart always ready to praise God for it.

Believing that God causes everything to work for our good turns our joy switch on. He wants to help us believe, but doesn't want to help us too much. If we see too much evidence that He is working, we may then begin to rely on evidence rather than learn to believe without evidence. In the next chapter we'll see a few occasions in which God gave me evidence, but only enough to encourage me onward.

FROM FEAR TO FAITH

Chapter 5

Yes, But What If?

My wife, Mary, and I visited Expo '86 in Vancouver. We did not expect the incredible things that happened when an "angel" took a special interest in our trip.

Everything we heard about Expo was good, except for the lo-o-o-ng lines for the best programs and the hours of waiting. Friends urged us to take folding chairs. "It's worth it," they encouraged, "but be prepared for aching feet." One young man told us that his feet had gone from numbness to a feeling of being stomped on by ten overweight elephants.

To me, standing that long would be aching, throbbing agony. I had endured miles of lines – twenty years of them – in military service. Frostbite, forced marches, and backbreaking loads had long since brutalized my feet, and they were vulnerable. My instant reaction to lines was fear bordering on panic. My fear said, "Stay away from Expo '86!" But I had learned new lessons about fear and how it can rob us of confidence and happy experiences.

What does going to a world's fair have to do with overcoming fear? I felt I should disregard my old fears and go to Vancouver as if I expected it to be a painless delight. With great determination I told myself, "Merlin, you will not be afraid of long lines."

I wrote for a booklet on bed-and-breakfast accommodations in Vancouver. We had enjoyed staying in private homes in England, and thought it would be interesting to do so in Canada. We selected one and took a taxi there. The family was delightful, telling us many things about Expo – and how long the lines would be!

The next morning we had a fabulous breakfast in the dining room, then took a forty-five-minute bus ride through the city. It was a sunny Friday in September, and we had folding chairs and books to read to cope with the tedious lines.

Secure in our confidence that God would work everything for our good, it had never occurred to us to pray for supernatural help. We were prepared to endure.

At the entrance, people moved in every direction. Millions of people, it seemed. We hadn't the faintest idea of where to go or how to get there. Lines seemed to reach for miles to all points of the compass, and we couldn't see where they started or ended.

All we could think of was, Thank You, Lord. Then the thought came: What good will come of all this? I knew of the marvelous Christian Pavilion at Expo, so I thought, perhaps You have all these people here for an opportunity to hear the good news.

My heart was at peace. Without striving to accept the situation or asking God to intervene, I was enjoying the moment. For sure, I hadn't reacted that way during my twenty years in the army. There I'd learned to be an expert complainer, but I knew now that the thousands of hours of standing in lines were in preparation for what God wanted to teach me.

The main line in front of us seemed to be one hundred miles long, and it wove back and forth at the British Columbia Pavilion. Great, I thought, here is a place we have been urged to see. We asked an employee: "What do we do?"

"Have you tickets for this pavilion?"

"No, where do we get in line?"

"Come back tomorrow morning at eight, and get in

the line marked 'Tickets.'"

"How long will it take to get them?"

"Probably an hour or more, but don't be late or you won't get tickets. Your tickets will be stamped with the hour you can see the program. Get into the pavilion line about two hours before it begins, or you may lose out."

Our heads spun a bit, but we were ready for the grand event however long it took.

Suddenly a man appeared and asked us if we would like two tickets. I expected to pay, thinking scalpers hadn't taken long to find us. Were they good ones, or were they counterfeits?

He handed them over, asked for nothing in return, then left.

The tickets were stamped for 10:50 a.m. Hey! That's the next program! We moved toward the pavilion sign that read "10:50 a.m. program," and soon found ourselves at the head of the line. I expected the attendant to say, "I don't know how you got these tickets, but they are counterfeit," and then to call the police. But in minutes we were in the theater for the film we'd heard so much about. We had been at Expo less than twenty minutes.

I've tried many times to understand why that man gave us those tickets. Who was he? Why did he disappear so quickly? The odds against anyone standing in line for hours to get tickets and then giving them to me are at least a million to one. I believe it was God who sent our benefactor.

The film of British Columbia's panoramic scenes was incredible.

It was lunchtime. We had been warned that food lines also were very long. At the nearby Saskatchewan Restaurant we saw about one hundred people in line. Since the Lord had already been so good to us, we were not too disappointed. But we decided to look for the restaurant that was located in the Ontario Pavilion instead. We took about fifty steps, and there it was, right in front of us.

Its walkway was an upward winding one about two hundred feet long, with no one in line. It must be closed, we thought.

But in moments we were shown to the last empty table, with a picture-window view of the fabulous inlet, False Creek. Ferries and cruise and pleasure boats bobbed under a gorgeous Canada sun. The meal was superb – close to perfect. When the Lord wants to especially bless us, He certainly knows how. He doesn't always provide exquisite meals for Mary and me; far from it. But at that special time He arranged to teach us important lessons.

I had a warm glow in my heart. I knew that God had intervened in our affairs, saying, "Merlin, I can do anything, any time, to meet any need you have. Don't ever be afraid."

I heard a couple at the next table speak of a marvelous three-dimensional film they had seen there in the Ontario Pavilion. It was a must-see, they said, echoing others. They had come to Expo an hour before it opened, and then waited in line three hours for the film Discovery. "Fantastic!" they said.

"Is it worth standing in line for three hours?" I asked.

"By all means! It's the most unusual film we have ever seen. Stand in line, however long it takes!"

Following their directions, we arrived at the Discovery Theater. There were only a few people around it. We just knew it couldn't be the right place. Hundreds of people would be in line. Mary asked an attendant if it was the place to line up. He said, "Yes, but this isn't the main entrance, and if you go into the theater this way, you can't see the preliminary exhibits." Those exhibits, we had been told, were the only part not worth standing in line for.

Ten minutes after our fabulous lunch we were in line for the film; then another extraordinary thing happened. Almost immediately the door opened, and we were shown to the best seats. Other people had waited three hours for seats, but we were inside in less than two minutes.

The three-dimensional film was indeed a discovery. Unforgettable. Breathtaking! The pictures seemed to leave the screen and move up to our faces. Geese in formation turned and seemed to fly right at us; a woman in front of us ducked her head. Did God love Mary and me more than the others? No. He had chosen that day to show us He could do anything, any time, anyplace. Our only obligation was to trust Him. If He knew I needed to stand in many lines over the course of many years, His love could arrange it, but only as a blessing. From those countless times of waiting in Army lines, I learned that it was special training for those of us who tend to be impatient.

The hours the Lord saved us from waiting in lines at Expo enabled us to have just enough time to visit the Pavilion of Promise. After a movie and live presentation, we were invited into a chapel, given a pamphlet with a gospel message, and led in a prayer of repentance. Each person was asked to raise a hand if he or she wanted to accept Jesus as Savior. The man in charge told us that every day hundreds of people raised their hands.

Those experiences reinforced my growing conviction that God wants to help us renounce any fears that might defeat His objectives. Soon I would learn another lesson in the power of faith that overcomes fear.

Midnight Calls

The piercing ring of the telephone forced my eyes open. The clock showed midnight.

"Merlin, I'm in a telephone booth in the middle of nowhere, and I can't find Genie. Have you heard from her?"

Telephone booth? Our daughter missing? What was Mary talking about? Why isn't Mary here? I struggled to awaken. Then I then recalled that she had left several hours earlier to be with our daughter while Genie delivered her third child.

Before Mary got there, our daughter-in-law, Shelly, had called the doctor. He was some forty miles away, and the delivery was scheduled to be in his office. The baby was due and saying, "I'm coming!" Genie had to get to the doctor's office immediately. They made a dash in that direction.

When Mary arrived at the doctor's office, his doors were locked and the windows dark.

I was wide awake. Fear made a bold attack on my heart. Where was our daughter? Had she been in an accident? Where was Mary? From what dark, lonely phone booth had she called? I had failed to ask her. What should I do?

For a long while I wrestled with my fears, then realized that if it is true that I can trust God, then I need not have fearful thoughts. I must remember how perfectly God works all things for our good.

Our daughter Genie did not make it to the doctor's office until after the birth. No accident, just the normal workings of nature. While Shelly was racing to get her there, Genie said, "It's too late; the baby's coming!"

"Coming! It can't come now. We are in the middle of nowhere."

"Sorry, but it's coming."

Our frantic daughter-in-law stopped at a gas station and asked for the nearest hospital.

"There's a little one up the road a piece."

Up the road apiece! They raced to the emergency entrance. "Help! Quick! A baby's coming."

"We have no facilities here for babies."

"But she's delivering now, in the car!" A startled doctor ran out. Genie was in the back seat of the car, taking pictures of the baby.

"Doctor, is it a boy or a girl?"

"If you would stop flashing the camera, I could see!"

Daughter and granddaughter were both well. There had been no need to be afraid. Genie said later that while on the wild car ride, she kept saying, "Thank You, Lord. I know You will use this for my good." And He did.

Fear of Sickness

My physical infirmities have often tempted me to have fearful thoughts. Each illness required me to accept one of two alternatives:

1. I'm sick and getting sicker.
2. I'm sick, but God is healing me.

The first was no option at all; I felt continually depressed.

As we grow older, negative thoughts become increasingly easier to adopt: If I'm hurting now, I'll surely hurt even more when I'm a few years older. What will happen to me when I get too ill to take care of myself? What happens when my money runs out and I can't work? Such thoughts could make every day miserable. Many older people are haunted by such dire speculations. So, readers of every age, please listen and heed.

Thoughts based on fear breed more of the same.

Thoughts based on faith in God result in peace and joy.

There was a time when a bad night's sleep would set me up for a bad day. It would begin with the thought: Today will be rough. Lack of sleep will make me tired all day. My day was controlled by my negative thoughts. Eventually I realized the foolishness of my attitude. Instead of expecting a bad day, I began to expect a good one. Lack of sleep could work *for* me instead of against me. To my joy, I've found that expecting the best consistently helps me to enjoy days that otherwise would be unpleasant.

My ninety parachute landings had exacerbated the arthritis in my spine. Such an ailment is a marvelous aid to self-pity and self-protection. I practiced worrying about how much weight I could lift without injuring my poor spine. I would pick up a twenty-five-pound item warily, and wonder if it would be too much of a strain. What a burden to have such fear!

If you have never suffered from spinal problems, you may not know how excruciatingly painful they can be. It is easy to live in fear that the pain might develop into endless misery. But I've learned that I can joyfully believe that God is caring for me.

You may have a totally different problem, but the solution is the same. Practice believing that God is healing your body or is solving your problems. Your faith will grow, and you will gradually – perhaps even rapidly – realize that He is creating a fresh new attitude in you: *God who gives you hope will keep you happy and full of peace as you believe in him. I pray that God will help you overflow with hope in him* (Rom. 15:13 TLB).

Let me share another personal experience. As a soldier, I was continually with men who took great pride in their physique. Unfortunately that attitude became part of my thought pattern too, without my even wanting to think that way. Part of me knew that physical strength had nothing to do with learning to trust God to supply our needs, but another part of me was proud of my excellent health.

As I grew older, it became crystal clear that my physical strength was declining. That did not mean that God loved me any less; it simply meant that Merlin was getting older. But I didn't like that, and sometimes I grumbled.

Recently I was doing the exercises I try to do every day. As I frequently did, I was bemoaning the fact that as the years go by, I can do less and less. Then I received an inner revelation: "Merlin, what you are thinking is not right. The reason you are losing your physical strength is that you are getting closer to the time when you will go to heaven!"

My attitude changed. I began to rejoice in the exercises that I could still do. For the first time in months, I was able to thoroughly enjoy the strength that God gives me.

Then I thought of something else. When I die, I will not be able to move any part of my body. No big revelation, I know. But when that happens to my body, I will actually be in heaven!

God may not give us perfect health, even though we might think He should. But flawless health is not necessarily a measure of our faith. Faith helps us to accept our present state of health, and to glory in our confidence that God always wants to work good in and for us. Even getting old can be a blessing! My exercise time has become more enjoyable to me now than it was when I was young and full of vigor.

If we believe that God is *not* working for our good, the body cooperates and says, "I agree! I feel terrible." The truth is, if God stopped all of the healing and restoration that is continually working in our bodies, we would soon die. A small cut in the skin could cause death. If God withdrew our capacity to sleep, we would soon be asleep permanently — in the grave.

If you break an arm, you would be wise to visit a physician who would x-ray the bone and set it. Then you could go on your way believing that your arm is healing.

But some infirmities are very different. The doctor may not know what to do, and we might feel helpless. We then have the opportunity to believe that God heals us by the same power that heals a broken bone.

James 1:6–8 tells us, *Let him ask in faith, with no doubting, for he who doubts is like a wave of the sea driven and tossed by the wind. For let not that man suppose that he will receive anything from the Lord; he is a double-minded man, unstable in all his ways.*

What most often causes us to doubt? Not seeing results.

At a meeting in San Antonio during the Persian Gulf War, I prayed with an army officer and his wife. He was discouraged and looked quite miserable. His back had been severely injured, and he was permanently off flying status. To a pilot, that is like telling him he has an incurable disease. His wife had a far worse problem. She had a cancerous growth in her breast and a tumor in her abdomen. As I prayed for them, there was no outward evidence of an immediate healing.

The next day the pilot reported to his army doctor and asked to be reexamined. Doctors regularly get this request from men who have been taken off flying status. This one told the pilot, "I'm sorry, but you will never again be able to fly for the Army." The man persisted; the doctor gave in and had X-rays taken of the "permanently" fused disks. The results confused the doctor but elated the officer. Nothing was wrong with his spine!

At home he told his wife, "We must get you back to your doctor. You may be healed also." She had another mammogram and an X-ray of her abdomen. All cancers were gone! Sometime later Mary and I met the couple during another series of meetings in San Antonio. At each service the beaming couple told everyone, "We are healed!"

When Mary and I pray for others, we always like to see immediate results, but God has taught us to pray and to leave the healing in His hands. Time after time people call or write us: "When you prayed, we felt nothing, but every day we keep feeling a little better." Often they have had serious infirmities for many years. After seeing this happen so often, Mary and I know that God honors prayers if we pray, believe, and keep on believing.

Too often Christians try to believe one way while feeling another way. Have you seen the dour-faced expression of one who says, "I have all kinds of faith, but nothing good happens"? It would be more correct for that person to say, "I do not believe God will answer my prayer; therefore, I feel miserable."

Many Christians develop a theological confession such as, "I'm supposed to believe that God is doing something for me; therefore, I believe He is." But a theological statement is not faith. When we *really* believe, we have *corresponding joy*.

Once we realize how crucial it is that we believe what we say, then we will concentrate on learning to believe. *We can learn.* This task may seem difficult, but it need not be. We can approach our goals with anticipation and gladness. We are working with the Holy Spirit to become more like Christ. In the next chapter, let's learn more about how to increase our faith.

51

Chapter 6

Learn and Believe

Believing requires learning. We can learn, one step at a time, to discard a lifetime habit of believing only what we see or feel. A moment of reflection will convince us that what we see and what we feel are often the complete opposites of what is true.

Consider the room or place in which you read this book. Is it still, or is it moving? Is the Earth moving, or still? The truth is that the place in which you sit whirls through space at thousands of miles per hour. Thus, what you feel or see is often very unreliable.

When you use your faith, you do not rely on what you see or feel. You say, "God, Jesus promised that if I believe, You would work healing in me." You can't see or feel the healing of a broken arm, but you can believe that it is happening.

God may heal you through doctors, or He may lead you to change your diet or perhaps to exercise more. There are various pathways to health. God may even work a miracle. But expect the miracle that *He* selects. Naaman expected a dramatic miracle, but when Elisha told him to wash in the Jordan River seven times, he was disgusted and thought Elisha was a fraud. *When Naaman finally heeded Elisha's advice, he was healed* (2 Kings 5:14).

You and I should accept God's healing through whatever means He selects. Our part is to believe, and to keep on believing. Jesus made a simple promise to us: *All things are possible to him who believes* (Mark 9:23).

Jesus' faith always produced instant miracles. Perhaps because of this, we Christians want our faith to work instantly, too. Some even demand that it do so. If it doesn't, they give up. Faith, however, often works gradually.

At a meeting in Maryland I prayed for a boy of ten. There were no obvious results. Neither the parents nor I could see any evidence of a miracle. Then, this letter came to me the next month:

"You prayed for our son Christopher at your meeting last month in Bel Air, Maryland. He was epileptic and mentally retarded. Just two days after that meeting, Chris brought home a note congratulating us on his improvement. After a year and a half at that special school, this was the first encouraging note we had received!

Now, for the first time in his ten years, Chris can go up and down stairs! He is happier and better in every way."

When we suffer severe pain, we normally want the quick relief offered by the shot of medication that a doctor gives. But quick solutions that are misused can eventually cause other problems, such as drug addiction. In most situations we need to seek more permanent solutions. Jesus gave us His solution when He said, *If you can believe, all things are possible to him who believes* (Mark 9:23). I'm convinced that He intended this statement to encourage us. We can grow in faith until our faith helps us solve any problem!

What if we have no known illness, but for some unknown reason we feel miserable? Most of us have days like that. Faith gives us the power to overcome our feelings, too.

Angels do not always appear. Prison doors do not always spring open. But believing *always* changes people. I have known people who lived in nightmares of suffering, but were transformed into creatures of joy when they turned their fears into faith.

If you suffer from some infirmity, I encourage you to tell God, "I believe You are healing me." Then continue to believe that He is. Don't look at the outward circumstances. If you don't feel better tomorrow, don't look upon that as failure. The body often feels extra sick when it is being mended.

Our feelings nearly always want to overpower our faith in God's promises. But sometimes there are hidden clues in the way we feel. If you pray for something good and believe you receive it, how do you feel? You feel happy! That is part of the reaction we always have when we expect something good. In the same way, we feel *unhappy* when we don't believe God is answering our prayers.

If you are convinced that your employer will never give you a raise, no matter how hard you work or how excellent your performance, how do you feel when you think about a raise? You don't believe you are going to get it, and you don't feel good about that.

If there is a possibility that your boss will raise your pay, but you only hope for it, do you feel good about it? A little nebulous, isn't it? Sometimes you expect it and you feel good, but at other times you expect never to get higher pay, and you feel bad.

If your employer says in writing, "Your work has been superior, and as of today you have a 25 percent raise," you feel great, even though you still do not have any extra dollars in your hands. Your *believing* and your *feelings* are in agreement.

Tell children that you will give them something they want, and see the expressions on their faces. They will express exactly what they believe will happen.

When you and I tell that God we believe He will answer our prayers, doesn't He see the expressions on our faces? More than that, doesn't He know exactly what is in our hearts?

For much of my life I'd been afraid to unite faith and feelings. I tried carefully to avoid any thought of how I happened to feel when I was trying to bolster my faith. Then one day I received a marvelous new insight that revolutionized my prayers.

Feelings should not control faith, but I had not learned the other part of this truth: *faith should control feelings*. As I learned to practice this principle, many of my old feelings were changed. It definitely wasn't easy. Old habits die hard.

Whenever my feelings controlled my faith, I noticed that I became discouraged. But the potential for change was so intriguing that I persevered. I learned that when I prayed for joy and peace, I needed to practice my faith by believing that God was indeed working good in me. As Jesus said, *These things I have spoken to you, that My joy may remain in you, and that your joy may be full* (John 15:11). Later He added, *These things I speak in the world, that they may have My joy fulfilled in themselves* (John 17:13). As I began to believe that God was working good in me, my feelings followed my faith. That inspired me!

The same principle applies when we pray for health. As we believe God is healing us, our feelings should say, "That's right! I *am* getting better!"

If we say, "I am discouraged because of this and this and this," we are mistaken. We are discouraged because our feelings are controlling our faith. Doubt brings discouragement and fear. Expectation brings delight.

If you have a miserable job, it will be even more so next month unless something changes. Chances are slim that the people you work with, or for, will change. But *you* can change. Practice dozens of times each day declaring that God is helping you to enjoy your work. Don't just say, "God, You are helping me to enjoy my work." *Believe* that He is.

"But my job is too horrible for anyone to enjoy," you may say. If Paul and Silas could enjoy heavy chains in prison, surely God is able to help us learn to enjoy our work. Many people will say that Paul did not enjoy his time in prison, for to them that would be ridiculous or impossible. But Paul said he had learned how to find joy in his troubles. If you find this difficult to understand, I encourage you to read my book, *Power in Praise*. It explains Paul's amazing discoveries regarding all things working for his good.

I do not suggest that you try to force yourself to enjoy your daily tasks. That would be akin to pulling yourself up by your bootstraps. Faith is different. It cooperates with God. It is believing that He is helping you to enjoy your employment and your life just as they are.

Jesus believed He was victorious when He was arrested and beaten. He claimed victory even when He was dying. Why was His belief so strong? He knew He would be resurrected. Death was absolutely necessary to His resurrection.

You and I can be victorious when faced with infirmities, problems, or suffering. Why? Because we, too, will be resurrected! And everything we experience in life prepares us for this.

Christ's tormentors mocked and challenged Him to come down from the cross if He was God. We will hear similar challenges echoing in our minds: If God is helping me, why doesn't He . . . ? But like Jesus, we can see by faith the joy that is set before us. Forever and ever we will rejoice with Him in our eternal victory.

Confess to God, "Today You are healing my body, my business, my marriage, or my problems. Your joy is filling my heart."

In Hebrews 11, God especially honors people who trusted Him. For dozens of years they patiently waited for answers to their prayers. Faith that works often needs to be practiced hundreds of times a day. God is healing me. This faith works for the man or woman who has a simple cold or for the person who is seriously ill.

The body can quickly heal a slight cut without assistance. A larger wound requires a bandage, anti-biotics, and much care. The body can heal a simple cold, but a serious illness may require medical aid, *and* faith.

Faith helps us get well; *God designed us that way.*

A child of nine months finds it difficult to walk, and needs encouragement to keep trying. He must try hundreds of times. Eventually he will run. Can he run a mile in four minutes? That takes more years of sometimes-painful discipline.

Faith, too, requires discipline: "God, You are taking care of this problem. I rejoice! I'm glad! I trust You! I will not hang my head in fear or worry! You are using this problem in some way to bless me! I am victorious!"

Jesus said to Martha: *Martha, Martha, you are worried and troubled about many things* (Luke 10:41). Some Christians are troubled about many things. But Philippians 4:4 says, *Rejoice in the Lord always.* "Always" means every minute. That's God's plan. It's the kind of faith that works healing and brings joy and happiness to those who choose trust in God instead of fear. Our objective is to be delivered from fears and to believe what we say we believe.

Consider the woman who came to Jesus with "a flow of blood" that caused her to suffer for twelve years (see Mark 5:25). Many doctors treated her, but she became worse, spent all her money, and had every reason to feel defeated. But she refused to give up. She heard about Jesus, and *she said, 'If only I may touch His clothes, I shall be made well'* (Mark 5:28). When she touched His clothing, she was made well. Why?

Before we answer, we should first hear Jesus' response to her. He said, *Your faith has made you well.* (Mark 5:34). But her own thoughts caused her to believe. She thought the right thoughts. My message throughout this book is simple: what you think is important!

Remember, the woman didn't even ask Jesus for help. She believed that if she touched Him, she would be well. The moment she combined believing and touching Him, the miracle happened.

It wasn't the touching that healed her. A thousand people might have touched Jesus' garments that day, for He was surrounded by people who were struggling to get near Him. Only this woman was healed. If we could touch Jesus' body today, we would receive nothing unless we also believed.

Many prayers for healing are lazy and unwise – like the farmer who asks God to sow his seeds. He wants good crops, but without toil.

We received this letter: "When you were in Cincinnati in April 1991, you prayed for my daughter. She is eleven, and has battled scoliosis, and a crooked back, for many years. She lived with continual pain. The day you prayed for her she had an immediate change – the pain decreased. Within two days her back was straight and she had no pain!"

My wife and I have had the joy of praying for thousands of people. The results? Some said they felt no improvement in their health or happiness. Some reported instant healing. But most said that a process began that caused their health and happiness to improve in ways that amazed them.

Do your best to be unaffected by symptoms, or by how long you have felt this way or that way. Be well in your spirit. Let Jesus' Spirit be yours. Let Him select the best way to honor your faith. Do this, and fear will disappear.

Now let's consider what fear can do to us and the marvelous changes that faith brings.

Chapter 7

Fear of Death

"You nearly scared me to death!" What is the source of this strange expression? Where did the idea arise that one could be frightened to death? Is fear really that powerful? Throughout history there have been reports of fear causing persons to die.

A French author, writing on the French Revolutionary period, told of such an incident. A prisoner was forced to extend his arm through a small opening in a wall. On the other side, his captors bound his hand and told him that blood was dripping into a pan from a cut in his finger. They pricked his finger with a pin and dripped warm water over it and into a pan.

They kept telling the prisoner how much "blood" he was losing. One captor said, "He has lost a quart! His heartbeat is slowing!"

The captors pretended to discuss his vital signs and excitedly described an increasingly weakened condition as the warm water dripped. The author of the account said the prisoner's heart began to respond to his fear. Finally he had a heart attack and died.

Fear can cause heart attacks. In military operations I have seen men so paralyzed with fear that muscles in their bodies would not move. Heart muscles could easily do the same. I have seen men prepare for combat with no apparent fear. They felt invincible. But many of the same men had a different attitude when they became seriously wounded. The possibility of life after death was then of paramount interest to them.

Life is a paradox. It seems to demand that we

cleave to it while simultaneously, requiring eventual surrender to eternity.

Seeing Life After Death

For many years I believed that to leave this earth and enter heaven would be glorious, but who wants to hurry it along? I felt a dread for the unknown that lay ahead – until one eventful night I looked through a window that opened into forever.

After many years with uneventful nights of sleep, I had a strange experience that changed my attitude toward life, death, and eternity. It all began suddenly one night when I felt suspended in midair near the ceiling in our bedroom. I looked down to see myself lying in bed. This is strange, I thought. No, it's impossible. No one will ever believe this!

Never had I encountered anything that even remotely compared with this event. It is hard to explain how I can be certain that some part of me was fully awake while my body was asleep.

Paul expressed a similar sense of confusion when he said, *Whether in the body I do not know, or whether out of the body I do not know, God knows* (2 Cor. 12:2).

The wide-awake Merlin Carothers was about twelve feet away from the "me" I saw on the bed. The thought came: How did I get up here?

I seemed to be suspended above and to the left of a beautiful, ever-changing scene that appeared to be about fifty feet away. As I looked, I saw a brilliant, flowing river, all the colors of the rainbow, plus what seemed to be an infinity of hues. Even more spectacular was the water itself. It was alive!

How to describe "living" water? It appeared to move within itself, revolving, sparkling, bubbling, dancing, almost seeming to laugh. I wanted to watch that water forever.

The grass on the bank appeared green, yet it, too, seemed to embody every color. Green one minute, then multicolored as it moved. We normally think of green grass as alive. But that grass was so much *more* alive. It seemed to move about in happy, effortless waves. The rows of multihued flowers were reminiscent of an orchestra, harmonious, flowing in rhythm.

Nearby were elegant, graceful trees that appeared to preside over the flawless panorama. They were "speaking," but I could not understand their words. Strength seemed to flow from them. Their fruit resembled nothing I had ever seen. The scene radiated joy and peace. I wanted to enter it and stay forever.

As I strove to move closer to the incredible scene, a power held me in a firm but gentle grasp. The more I struggled, the more firmly I was held back.

"Not yet, Merlin," came a voice of authority and strength. I knew I should not resist it, and I was slowly pulled away. It was unbearable to think of leaving, but then I awoke, and it was daylight.

I have known people who waged gallant battles to stay alive until just a few minutes before death. They saw something so beautiful, they wanted to reach out to claim it. But those persons were gone so quickly that I could never learn what they had seen.

Back to Earth

I walked to the window as I did every morning. The hills and lush green valley around our home were as beautiful as ever. But that morning something seemed wrong. Our beautiful hills and valley looked dead. The scene no longer held any magic for me. What had changed? Only my perspective.

That entire day I was in a daze. I knew I had experienced something that was changing me. In contrast to my vision, the world around me seemed faded and worn. My attitude toward death was changed. I knew that someday I would plunge into that same living water I had seen. Oh, Death, what joy you will bring!

I looked up Bible references. I had never questioned the meaning of the living water Jesus described to John in Revelation 7:17: *The Lamb . . . [will] lead them to living fountains of waters. And God will wipe away every tear from their eyes.*

I don't know how to interpret all I saw, but I understand that life after death will introduce us immediately to the real, living world. The things we see here on our planet are damaged and polluted. Every animal and plant struggles to stay alive. Everything is in the process of dying. But our next world is eternal. God's plan for us is breathtaking! One tiny glimpse filled my heart with expectation. I can't tell you *why* He gave me that glimpse. Perhaps it was for you.

You may be wrestling with problems, and thinking, Will they never end? Oh, yes. Even now they are in the process of fading away and dying. But in eternity, everything is designed to increase in beauty and strength and purity. How can perfection increase in perfection? I don't know, but I will enjoy learning.

The vision I saw enlarged my understanding of the lack of importance of this present world. Everything we see and touch is passing away. Even Satan will one day be gone. Until then, when difficulties confront you, remember that Satan wants you to think that things are bad and getting worse. The truth is that things are bad and getting worse for him.

When Jesus was here, He evaluated everything as

to its true worth. He compared one hundred years of life on earth with eternity as a mere blink of an eye. I am growing in understanding this. My vision of the living water, grass, flowers, and trees was a mere sip at the fountain of living water. All of that will serve only as background to the dazzling, magnificent presence of God.

I wondered if the vision would lead to new understanding. It came some months later.

I was asleep, but barely. A severe pain along my spine broke my restless slumber. As I turned from side to side in those predawn hours, I wrestled with my persistent problem: Why do I hurt so much? Why doesn't God heal me as He has done at other times? For how long can this pain intensify? Have my days of usefulness ended?

Then I heard an inner voice: You aren't filled with joy, Merlin.

"No, Lord, I am not. I can't be. I hurt too much."

Yes, you can.

So I began to say, "Thank You, Lord, for this pain." After a few minutes of praising Him, the pain was the same, but I felt a glimmer of hope. I praised Him for the gift of eternal life and the joy of knowing Jesus as my Savior.

The sun had not yet lightened the day, but a new joy blazed in my heart. Just before daybreak, I opened my Bible to Revelation 22:1. I had quoted it often: *And he showed me a pure river of water of life* (Living water!).

I realized the extraordinary blessing that God had given me. But I would not have received that realization if I had not praised my way from discouragement to joy in my battle with pain. Thousands of times I had felt sorry for myself without realizing that my self-pity did nothing to help me receive something good.

Now I believe the Lord helped me so I could help you when you face your own hours of pain. Don't be discouraged, ever!

Receiving Good Things

I've often failed to receive good things because I misinterpreted Isaiah 40:31: *Those who wait on the Lord shall renew their strength.* To me, waiting meant having patience until God came and did something for me. As He renewed my strength, it became clear what waiting means. It is in the same sense as a waiter serving in a restaurant. He doesn't sit around until the customer pays him. No, he serves him. Waiting on God means serving Him. When I actively praised God for His blessings to me, I served Him. That prepared the way for Him to renew my strength. But my service had to be done in joy. It's rather difficult to convince God that I'm joyful if I'm really not.

If you are experiencing difficulties, I urge you to find opportunities to serve, to wait on God. You don't need to quit your job and become a paid, full-time minister. Serve Him by doing what you can to help the people around you. Serve your spouse, your neighbors, or the people with or for whom you work. Remember these two significant details:

1. *Inasmuch as you did it to one of the least of these . . . you did it to Me* (Matt. 25:40).
2. *Serve the Lord with gladness* (Ps. 100:2).

For then you shall *obtain joy and gladness, and sorrow and sighing [complaining] shall flee away* (Isa. 35:10).

A martyr's attitude accomplishes little or nothing. Service needs to come from a joyful heart.

If we just endure our painful situations, we may feel

spiritual, but God wants to use them to help us grow spiritually. Self-pity is as dangerous to spiritual maturity as poison is to the body.

Most of us have had considerable practice at thinking, Why did this have to happen to me? The fallen part of our nature seems inclined to concentrate on our problems. It is susceptible to dwelling upon things that are painful and fearful.

God made us capable of thinking about good and lovely things. We must learn to choose to think His thoughts rather than anxious, fearful thoughts.

Have you ever awakened in the morning thinking, *oh, no, it's time to get up*? It's easy to entertain such unhappy thoughts. You may feel that your life couldn't be worse. You have needs in every area, and nothing is getting better. The fallen nature loves to moan about everything. The older you get, the more automatic your negativity becomes. But God has a better way.

Philippians 4:19 declares, *My God shall supply all your need according to His riches in glory by Christ Jesus.* Many people apply a negative twist to this verse, with the emphasis on the "shall supply." They think that as long as God has not yet supplied their needs, they still have a right to be unhappy. That verse was written nearly two thousand years ago and has been in force ever since. God does supply our needs now. Right now is the moment in which we are to rejoice. We have exactly what we need. Until we learn that, we cannot receive the blessings from God that we desire, and fear is always there to push its way into every situation.

Tomorrow, next week, or a month from now, you may feel distressed. When that occurs, remember what you have learned. God's desire is that you enter His promised land. He created you with the physical, emotional, and spiritual need to live in peace. Ask any physician. Unhappiness causes stress in every organ of the body. When unhappiness becomes severe enough, the body can react with sickness or even death.

Jesus, however, told us that God offers us a new opportunity to be unencumbered with the disease of unhappiness.

Grumbling

God told the Israelites to stop grumbling, complaining, and being unhappy. They refused. As an object lesson to all future generations, He caused two to three million of them to die in the desert. Only two men of that generation made it into the promised land. Consider those odds!

How many Christians do you know who do not regularly grumble and complain? Like the Israelites, we may have plenty of excuses, but God says no excuses are acceptable. He designed us for joy, and He sacrificed His Son to help us find it. Now it's up to us. If we prefer to disobey and live in unhappiness, the decision is ours, but we will fail to experience the incredible joy that comes as we grow to trust God more and more. Hebrews 4:1 (TLB) tells us to tremble with fear because some of us may be on the verge of failing to enter into His place of rest.

Reading this book could be your means of becoming the Caleb or Joshua who enters the promised land. If you have wasted precious energy thinking of your physical or emotional pains, try from this moment on to think new thoughts. You will be surprised and pleased to see how the Holy Spirit helps you to have a new song in your heart.

The disciples practiced what they preached. Imprisoned, they sang at midnight. Then, great joy filled their thoughts and hearts. Like a fountain, it spilled over into the cold, dark cell. How did they do that? They did it through Christ.

God's Plans

God's goal is to prepare us to fellowship with Him for eternity. We must spend this life learning what we need to know. Otherwise we will not be equipped for our position and purpose in eternity. If I expend my energies praying for things I shouldn't have, God would defeat His own plans by honoring such prayers. Though our present bodies are frail, God decided that they perfectly suit His purpose. He takes our temporary bodies and uses them as places to work good in our eternal spirits.

I've learned that the most difficult task I must perform is to put God's plans first: *Seek first the kingdom of God* (Matt. 6:33). Our natural instinct is to take care of our families, our churches, and our friends. Jesus' nature was to care for the people others shunned. At the end of this life, we will be judged according to the measure of our love for God and for people. It will profit us nothing to tell God about the sins we haven't committed or the miracles we have experienced. If we love ourselves too much, we will have little time and strength to love others.

Get It Done Yesterday

I'll share a truth with you that's worth one hundred times what you paid for this book.

Life often pressures us with the feeling that we must get things done immediately – if not sooner. Pressure can make us tense, irritable, resentful, and confused.

Sometimes we race as fast as we can go; other times we may become discouraged, give up, and do nothing.

For many years I was accustomed to handling pressure in these ways until I heard a voice within: Merlin, you have only one thing to do – please Me. That was a revelation to my oft-troubled spirit. I had nothing else to do but please God. Now I remember and obey that message several times every day.

When I have a task to do that seems too time consuming, I remember that I have only one thing to do. When I feel pressured by some responsibility or some frustration, I'm able to rejoice when I remember that I can please God if I do my task with a joyful spirit.

Then I learned that *now* is the time I should please God. Not after a while. Not when I complete some task – now. When I center my attention on pleasing Him now, other responsibilities fade into the background. It is now that He wants me to be filled with peace.

One of the men on a cross beside Jesus could think only of his own physical condition. He had no interest in pleasing God now. So he challenged Jesus: "Get me off this cross!" The other man had a higher goal. His pain was just as great, but he asked Jesus to remember him when they entered the next world. His goal was right, and Jesus promised him he would attain it.

Remember these two men. The first asked for help to get off his cross, and he received nothing. The second asked to enter Christ's kingdom, and he received eternal life. Jesus didn't ask either of them to change his past, to do anything for Him, or to promise to do anything in the future. Both men needed help, but each had different priorities. One focused his attention on his physical needs; the other sought the highest attainable goal - to be remembered in Jesus' kingdom.

You may find yourself as helpless as the thief on the cross. It may seem that you can do nothing to help yourself. This often results in fear.

Most men would like to be strong, but for some, building muscles is a top priority. Most women would like to be beautiful, but some make it their top priority. If our priorities are out of balance, we are in spiritual jeopardy.

Putting the wrong things first is dangerous. God would like our physical bodies to be healed and all our problems solved. But He never puts our bodies first. No matter what we request or what anyone tells us, our spiritual needs will always be most important to God.

God wants a bride for Christ that is without spot or wrinkle. A perfectly healthy body, unfortunately, might lead us in the opposite direction. When we think we have everything we need, we often have no great desire for God's help. That isn't God's fault or His choice. It is ours.

If a physician tells me I will die, the person I am at that moment determines how I will react. If death means I will lose everything that I have put first, I'm in bad shape. Serious illness is a master at creating fear. But it cannot defeat my faith in God if I have learned to put His will first. My body is not my first priority; therefore, it doesn't control me. Death becomes eternal joy, and therefore works for my good. There is no way I can lose.

Jesus considered our priorities our most prized attributes. The rich young man who came to Him had a priority – money. Jesus told him to sell everything and give the money to poor people. That was too much for a man whose money had first place in his heart.

People who are blind often go through a time of

intense discouragement. Healing could easily become their priority. I can understand that. But one man, Sydney Scroggle, achieved something that still stirs my enthusiasm. I copied one of his statements in my notebook, but I failed to list the title of his book or other important details about his life. I evidently believed and was blessed by what he wrote. I give you his quotation with the hope that it will encourage you in your efforts to have faith that God is working for good in your life. Scroggle wrote, "I came eventually to adopt an attitude towards blindness, resulting in freedom from all sense of restriction, feelings of self-pity, resentment, or embitterment. I cannot get anyone to believe me, but as others rejoice in their sight I rejoice in my blindness. It is purely and simply my own idea, that I would choose, had I a thousand alternatives." I am sure that Sydney struggled through and learned many things before he reached the freedom he describes.

A Hospital in Vietnam

When I was a chaplain in Vietnam, wounded men were airlifted by helicopter to the evacuation hospital. This hospital differed from those you have visited. Buildings were of hastily erected corrugated metal, arranged in half-moon design, sitting on the ground or on cement slabs. Row after row of huts were full of wounded men. We received them within hours after they were injured.

War is a humbling experience, stripping most people of the smug pretenses they may have. The awesome experience of war and the ever-present reality of death brought people face-to-face with themselves and their enemy, fear.

When I saw each casualty for the first time, I had no idea how serious his wounds might be. I might see only a small hole in the skin, made by a tiny fragment of steel. But appearances can be deceptive. The injury that didn't look like much could by the next morning be fatal.

As I stood by the bed of each newly arrived soldier, I realized that whatever I said might be the last words he would hear. I had no way of knowing what he needed most to hear, or what his spiritual priorities had been. Many men were afraid; some were terrified. If a medical team was approaching, I knew it would be seconds before I had to leave.

Whatever I said needed to be exactly the right words. At times I sensed that my words expressed just what the particular soldier wanted to hear. As I went from bed to bed, I grasped each man's hand or touched some part of his body, telling him that I was there to help. If he were strong enough, he would grip my hand. He might never have attended chapel, but he wanted to talk with someone who, to him, represented God. I was then able to tell him of the times I, too, had been afraid, and how I found peace through my faith in Jesus.

I spent most of my time at the EVAC hospital at the men's bedsides. Time after time I led men into personal relationships with Christ. The horror and stress of battle are long remembered, and I believe the survivors often recall how their faith in God caused their fear to leave.

During those days I developed a passionate desire to help you be delivered from any stranglehold that fear may have on you. Faith in God defeats, then destroys, all kinds of fear.

Now let us consider the different methods by which God urges us to believe Him.

FROM FEAR TO FAITH

Chapter 8

A Man of Great Faith

Jacob Van Gorder was born in New Jersey in 1761. In 1777, he was in the battle of the Tories and Native Americans against the settlers in Wyoming Valley, Pennsylvania. Native Americans captured him, but then a Native American woman adopted him as her son and saved his life.

After living with them for five years, he escaped while on a hunting party. Jacob is my ancestor; his genes are a part of me.

My father, David, is still a part of my physical and spiritual makeup. He had never been confined to bed even one day until he died at age thirty-six. He had a beautiful wife and three healthy young sons. In his final year of laboring in the U.S. Steel Mill in Ellwood City, Pennsylvania, he was the highest-paid hourly worker among the thousands there.

Father's closest friend told me this unusual story: "The Sunday evening before your father died, he lingered at the church altar even after the lights were turned off. Finally only he and I were there. I said to him, 'Dave, do you have a problem?' He answered: 'I'm telling God that if necessary, I'm willing to die in order that my three sons might be saved.'"

A few days later my father died of pneumonia.

Those final days of his life profoundly influenced Mother. She knew that an angel had appeared to him just before he died, and that in some way his prayer for his three sons was important.

I was twelve years old when Mother came home

from the hospital to tell us boys that our father was dead. For the first time in my life I felt the kind of fear that can paralyze emotions. Even now I cannot describe how utterly alone I felt. I didn't cry or talk with anyone.

In our community the custom was to have the deceased at home in an open casket while for three days relatives and friends came to view the remains. Those days stand out in my mind as the worst of my life.

The open casket was in the living room that I had to pass through many times each day. Often no one was there but me and my lifeless father, and the sight of his corpse gave me nightmares for years to come. I don't recall seeing the flowers around the casket, but I do remember the smell of roses. To this day, when I smell roses, my mind flashes back to that scene so many years ago.

After the funeral, Mother said we couldn't pay the rent on our house and we would have to move.

Dad had an old car, but to me it was the most magnificent chariot on the road. He had let me sit in his lap to steer, and he promised me a driver's license when I turned sixteen. When he worked on that old car, I always had my head in the way so I could see what he was doing. With his death, Mother had more bad news for us. The car had to go. She had no money for gasoline at twenty cents per gallon.

Such events as these were too terrible for my young mind to accept. First Dad. Then the house. When we had to let the car go, I wondered what would be next. I soon found out. Mother said we must be very careful of the food we ate so we wouldn't run out.

I kept my eye on the kitchen and wondered if we would have something to eat for the next meal. Somehow we always managed to have cornmeal and beans, served with Mother's love, but to sons who were fearful and insecure.

I am sure that some of my readers have endured even more difficult times, but I share these experiences so you will know that I, too, know how it feels to be afraid. As you read this book, you may understand why you have often felt fearful.

Golden Opportunities

At age fifteen, I found my world centered on playing football, baseball, basketball, hunting, and a growing speculation about what girls were all about. At times I felt a stirring within me urging me to seek God. I reacted as do many young people – I tried to keep Him from interfering with my life. To me, religion was for old people.

Yet, in one way or another, God kept sending this word to me: Merlin, you need to know Me. One day I began to seek Him, and soon I wanted the whole world to know Him. He had released in me an enthusiasm that overcame my inclination to be quiet and retiring.

When I attended church and the pastor said something that excited me, I would shout, "Praise the Lord!" unaware of what others around me were thinking. Later I learned of the disapproving comments some of the churchgoers made about my "vulgar display."

Fear of what people might say or think entered my heart. Then I learned the terrible secret: if I kept quiet, no one cared what I believed. My spiritual battle with fear had begun. Eventually I stopped speaking to anyone about Jesus. Revelation 2:4 was written for me: *I have this against you, that you have left your first love*. From age nineteen to age twenty-one I became a prodigal son and strayed far from God.

In my first book, *Prison to Praise*, I describe how God spoke to me when I was twenty-one. He said, *Tonight you must make a decision for Me. If you don't, it will be too late.* He was giving me my final opportunity to stay out of even more serious trouble than I had already experienced. I said yes, and He returned me to His service.

If you haven't been delivered from fearful thoughts, there's a very good chance that you, too, may be missing golden opportunities to influence others to accept Jesus as Savior. Your fear may be excused in several ways:

- I don't know how.
- People would reject whatever I said.
- I'm naturally shy.
- I'm not trained.

I recall an incident that impressed itself forever on my mind. When I held the lowly rank of private in World War II, I was once in a formation with forty-eight men. We were practicing the rifle manual of arms. Lieutenant Milam, a West Point graduate, shouted, "Right shoulder, arms; port arms; present arms." We had been trained to fear all officers. One of them could say, "Sergeant, make that private work all weekend." Or worse, "That private disobeyed my direct order. Put him in the stockade."

Abruptly, Lieutenant Milam gave us "at ease." He was clearly upset by our performance. He said, "You men act as if you are too tired to move your eyeballs. What's wrong with you? Put some life into what you're doing. Be proud you are paratroopers!"

Then: "There is only one of you who does this right. I'll bring him up here to show the rest of you lazy troopers the way it should be done."

Every man must have had the same thought: Who

is he talking about?

"Private Carothers, come up here!" he boomed in what I thought was an unnecessarily loud voice. I had to obey, but my feet didn't want to move. No sergeant, let alone an officer, had ever pointed me out as doing the manual of arms in an exemplary manner. Something terrible was about to happen.

With great trepidation I ran to the front of the formation, expecting any minute to hear him laugh and say, "Carothers, you are a perfect example of the soldier who does this all wrong!"

However, he had me demonstrate all the elements of the drill, with flattering comments on my performance. I was in shock. It did not occur to me that I handled the rifle in a special way.

From then on, lieutenants were not to be feared. Rifle drills became fun. Every soldier in the platoon watched to see how I did it, and the platoon sergeant looked on with obvious satisfaction. Lieutenant Milam was my hero, and I strove to please him.

That incident tells me that we are often needlessly afraid, and when fear enters our minds, it may take a dramatic experience to set us free of it. This has happened to me many times, as this book illustrates.

If someone had asked, "Carothers, do you care whether the officer in charge likes the way you do the manual of arms?" my answer would have been, "Do I care? Of course not." But I did care.

As you tell someone about eternal life, you want him or her to react with pleasure and to show delight in listening to such a wonderful person as you. But you may also be afraid of how the person may react.

Matthew gave us an unusual report about a man who was not afraid: *When Jesus heard it, He marveled, and said to those who followed, 'Assuredly, I say to you, I have not found such great faith, not even in*

Israel!' (Matt. 8:10).

Where did God's Son find the man of such great faith? His was not an occupation in which one would expect to find such faith. He was a soldier. Not Jewish, but Roman!

At age twelve, Jesus talked with the most religious people of His day. He later attended weddings, banquets, funerals, and talked with people wherever He went. But in all of Israel He had not met even one whose faith equaled that of the Roman soldier. What manner of man was he?

When Jesus located this soldier, He said, *I have not found such great faith*, indicating that He had searched. To others, He said, *How is it that you have no faith?* (Mark 4:40); and *O you of little faith* (Matt. 6:30).

For many a day after that, the Roman officer surely was the subject of conversation among all those who followed Jesus. They must have asked, "Why is his faith so strong and ours so weak? How can we get more faith?"

I have heard many sermons about this Roman centurion. The emphasis is usually on his believing that Jesus did not need to go to his home in order to heal his servant. That was unusual faith, but there was a much stronger dimension of the soldier's faith. He called Jesus "Lord" (Greek, kurios). The primary use of this word in the New Testament is reliance upon Christ for salvation.

Roman law decreed that the emperor was lord, and all persons were to place their faith in him. At the very least the officer had subjected himself to possible loss of his military rank. Worse, he could have been executed as a traitor for what he had said.

This Roman soldier had every reason to deny Jesus as Lord. His position as a centurion meant wealth and power. If you have neither, you can hardly know how challenging it is for people to relinquish them. Power is usually difficult to attain, but even more difficult to abdicate. People often will sacrifice health, family, and integrity to gain and keep power.

The centurion probably spent years working to attain his status. Yet by speaking a few favorable words about Jesus, he had laid himself open to lose everything. He had risked everything, but for what? Not for personal gain. He didn't need healing for himself or his family. He wasn't seeking status. He only wanted his servant to be healed.

In our culture that may not seem like a big thing, but the servant of a Roman was expendable. Servants had value, but they lived solely for their owner's convenience.

When you and I tell someone about our faith in Jesus, what do we jeopardize? Loss of earthly possessions? Or do we just risk being slightly embarrassed?

What caused the centurion to risk so much? Why was he unafraid when we are so often controlled by fear?

Jesus looked into the officer's heart and saw "great faith." We might miss the importance of what Jesus said if we do not understand the specific word He chose: Faith. What was the "great faith" that the officer had? The twelve disciples had already been out working miracles, yet not one of them was recognized as having great faith. There is no indication in the account that the officer had done any work of faith. His faith was of a far superior variety. What was it?

Jesus said He had not found such great "pistis". In Greek, pistis means "conviction of the truthfulness of God." It is used here to mean believing in Christ for salvation. Pistis is used in this context throughout the New Testament.

Jesus said to the centurion, A*s you have believed*

[pisteuo], so let it be done to you (Matt 8:13).

Many people believed that Jesus could work miracles, but those who came seeking them didn't impress Him. It was the centurion who was willing to risk his life by publicly announcing that he believed in Him as Lord who impressed and delighted Jesus.

There is more evidence that Jesus praised the centurion's faith in Him as Savior. In the next verse He said that, *many will come from east and west, and sit down with Abraham, Isaac, and Jacob in the kingdom of heaven* (Matt. 8:11). Jesus would never have promised heaven to a man for simply believing that He could heal his servant. The eternal plan of salvation is based on one thing only: faith in Jesus as Savior!

Not only did the Roman centurion *believe* in Jesus, he was happy to witness to his faith as well. His confidence in Jesus, and his willingness to express his faith openly, marked him as one who believed more than any other man on earth! That touched Jesus so much that He marveled – considering it wonderful and astonishing.

Keeping Quiet

I have never told anyone that I am not a Christian. But because of fear I often fail to express my faith. I find reasons strong enough to convince myself to keep quiet. I would have acknowledged Jesus as Lord many times if my heart had not headed a whisper from the demon of fear.

After Paul had been in prison for what some scholars believe to have been five years, he had good reason to hold his tongue. But he knew his mission, and was prepared to die rather than be silent. He was cast into prison for another five years. Ten years in a squalid dungeon would dampen the enthusiasm of any man.

Back on the streets, Paul still had but one message: Jesus is our only hope of eternal life! He is alive! I saw Him with my own eyes! He is Lord! Paul's trials had not defeated him.

Back to prison he went for five more years. Fifteen or more years there did not change Paul's passion to tell the world about his Savior.

For nearly two thousand years people have searched for evidence that the New Testament record is not based on fact. Microscopic searches have been made through every scrap of material, with no flaw found. Not one! Unbelievers have ranted and raved, insisting, "Jesus couldn't have risen from the dead." But He did! Jesus was the only One ever to conquer death.

Many people saw Christ in the forty days after His resurrection. Those who proclaimed the holy event were beaten, tortured, stoned, fed to the lions, or crucified. But they refused to recant. They were monumental proof that we serve a resurrected Jesus. Their sacrifice should inspire us to spread the news that He *is* alive.

In my lifetime, dozens of discoveries have verified the accuracy and reliability of the Bible. The media rarely report such revelations, but if one scrap of evidence were found to discredit Scripture, you can be sure that every branch of the news would feature it. Indeed, if after two thousand years people found even one such fact, that would be news.

Unrelenting efforts are made to show Jesus as just another man. The apostles, however, did not risk their lives preaching about just a good man. Jesus had the power to resurrect Himself from the dead, and they knew no ordinary man could do that.

Throughout history many men have promised to return from the dead, but not one has escaped the grave. Jesus was murdered, and just as He promised,

He was raised from the dead. He appeared to hundreds of people, and as one astonished group watched, He ascended and disappeared into the sky.

He had said that He would never leave them, but now He was gone. Those who had believed Him were in confusion. Some went back to their old jobs. Others met in small groups to await the possibility of further miraculous incidents. They did not know for certain what they waited for.

Then something happened! On the day of Pentecost, the church was born. Through the Holy Spirit, Jesus returned in a way that released the disciples from fear. Those who believed in Him were charged with new power and a surge of passion to spread the joyful news. Those who had been afraid were afraid no longer. They rushed to tell the world, "He is alive! He is alive!"

Many believed them. Hundreds, then thousands of new believers rushed to tell others. Excited throngs poured out of Jerusalem, telling travelers, fishermen, soldiers – everyone who would listen – that Jesus was alive.

Roman authorities saw that things were getting out of hand. Only Caesar was to be considered a god; Only he was to be worshipped. Commands went out. Anyone who claimed that Jesus Christ was alive would be fed to the lions. Many believers were murdered, but a strange thing happened: When two believers were slain, four would take their place. *Nothing* seemed to stop them.

But eventually something did! New believers became afraid to tell anyone the good news. Persecution decreased. Believers relaxed. No need to stir up trouble.

But the good news survived. Stronger and bolder Christians persisted in passing along the secret. One day you and I heard it. When we did, God sowed a seed in our hearts that enables us to be a part of His miracle. Working with Him we accomplish the impossible!

Hudson Taylor, one of the greatest missionaries of all time, said, "There are three stages in every great work of God. First, it is impossible, then it is difficult, then it is done."

Multitudes of Christians become tongue-tied when they have an opportunity to share Christ with unbelievers. Their desire to avoid the problems that may result from speaking up about Christ is stronger than their desire to communicate.

Christians often berate themselves unmercifully for failing to obey Christ. They feel defeated, discouraged, and wonder why they are such miserable examples of true discipleship. They read books about witnessing, attend classes, listen to sermons, but the problem remains unresolved.

What is wrong? The basic cause is not being considered – only the symptoms.

We can pray 10 times a day, 365 days a year for 50 years, for the strength to be a faithful witness, and still fail. Why? Because we allow ourselves to be divided. Jesus said, *[A] house divided against itself will not stand* (Matt. 12:25).

God has given each of us the power to cast out our fear of witnessing. We may need to exert this power over and over until we grasp the meaning of these verses: *If the Son makes you free, you shall be free indeed* (John 8:36) and, *Where the Spirit of the Lord is, there is liberty* (2 Cor. 3:17).

It doesn't take too much persuasion for most of us to muster up a good strong desire for an ice-cream sundae. By applying God's Word we can learn to *desire* to tell others about our Savior. The desire to build God's kingdom and the desire to stand back and escape responsibility are mutually exclusive. Waiting for someone else to initiate action usually indicates a lack of confidence in ourselves and in God. We can pray every day for confidence, but never feel it. Self-confidence is often unable to overcome fear, but unfailing confidence will come as we learn to cast fear from our hearts and minds.

Obedience

We Christians can lose spiritual battles because we let a spirit of defeat control our actions rather than stand on God's promises. We may repeat the verse, "I can do all things," over and over again. Sing it, pray it, even try to live it, but we will fail if we dwell in a "house divided against itself." Faith living in one room, but fear controlling the rest of the house.

The power of Christ's life rested in His decision to follow God's will. It was His obedience to God that provided our salvation. It is *our* obedience to Him that makes us workers with Him.

When people first began to report that Jesus was alive, they gave their testimonies so fearlessly that unbelievers knew if they became believers, they, too, would go about telling others of the power of Jesus to save. All too often that's not true today. Many Christians have been infected by the timorous behavior of other Christians; They become content to be secret believers. The results are tragic. Many converts never know the joy of telling others the good news, and their gladness of heart quickly dissipates.

Place a drop of blue ink in a glass of water, and the entire contents will turn blue. Just one drop. If we let one drop of fear infect our heart, it will permeate everything in us. Therefore, we must find ways to eliminate those drops of fear.

Chapter 9

Don't Be Manipulated

When people don't believe that God is actively involved in their lives, they find endless reasons to be afraid. If their faith in God declines, they then dwell on their fears.

Unbelievers scoff that Christians are being gullible when they place their confidence and trust in a God they can't see. So let's think about what we *can* see.

Picture the sky divided into thousands of windows the size of the moon as we see it from earth. With a giant telescope, let's zoom in and examine one of these windows. If our telescope is powerful enough, we will see not only individual stars, but galaxies too.

How many stars are in each galaxy? Astronomers say that there are one hundred billion to five hundred billion.

This reality staggers our mind, but The distance between the stars is even more incredible!

Consider a "short" trip from the earth to the *nearest* star, excluding the sun. If we could travel there by car on a smooth highway, and we averaged one thousand miles a day, it would take us millions of years to get there.

Other stars are 20 billion light-years away from earth, each distance equal to 186,000 miles per second, times 60 seconds per minute, times 60 minutes per hour, times 24 hours per day, times 365 days per year, times 20 billion years. Astronomers recently announced a supercluster of galaxies that are

6.5 billion light-years away from earth, and more than 500 million light-years across! The vastness of God's Creation is indeed incredible!

Impossibly huge and complex galaxies whirl in perfect harmony through this vastness, at tens of thousands of miles per hour. How many galaxies are there? Images received from the Hubble Space Telescope in 1996 reveal that there are at least fifty billion – five times the number previously estimated.

Consider that. Fifty billion galaxies! If each one contains one to five hundred billion stars, the total number of stars in the known universe is unimaginably astronomical!

Yet atheists dismiss the incredible vastness and impenetrable complexity of God's Creation as mere happenstance. These billions upon billions of galaxies with their uncountable trillions of stars, simply came into being "by accident," they insist.

Then consider the infinitesimal atom. This invisible particle is itself comprised of even smaller particles, i.e., electrons, protons, and a nucleus. These components, each a micro-universe, equal in complexity to the macro-universe of which they are a part, form matter, of which you and I and everything everywhere are comprised.

Ask an atheist to explain the origin of our indescribably vast and complex universe. While the mind of man is awesomely creative, he has, paradoxically, never created anything. He merely, rearranges the material (matter) created by God.

Proponents of evolution insist that everything merely "evolved." To believe that the universe simply appeared out of nothing seems to require a kind of imagination that is beyond comprehension. There had to be a Creator!

Even after I became a Christian I spent years

pleading with the Creator to show Himself: "God, why don't You reveal Yourself? Don't You want us to trust You? Why do You keep us in the dark?" The more doubt I expressed, the stronger it became. Doubt begets more doubt.

Then God ignited a spark of faith in me, and challenged me to do something with that spark. I could let it go out, or I could fan it into a flame that would release more faith. Now I know it is illogical to doubt God's existence. The belief that He created all things is the only rational conclusion that any thoughtful person can ever reach. It's no wonder that we want to shout to the world, "God is for real!"

Paul's faith in God was so strong that he continued to preach even when he knew his message could cause him to be cast into prison, even executed. His faith gave him the power to write chapters in the book that was to be published by God. Noted scholar H. L. Hastings wrote:

"Infidels for 1,800 years have refuted and over-thrown this book, and yet it stands today as solid as a rock. Its circulation increases, and it is more loved, cherished, and read today than ever before. Infidels, with all their assaults on this book, make about as much impression on it as a man with a tack hammer would on the pyramids of Egypt. When the French monarch proposed the persecution of Christians in his dominion, an old statesman and warrior said to him, 'Sire, the Church of God is an anvil that has worn out many hammers.' So, for ages the hammers of infidels have been pecking away at this book, but are now worn out and the anvil still endures. If it had not been the book of God, men would have destroyed it long ago. Emperors and popes, kings and priests, princes and rulers have all tried their hands at it; they die and the book still lives."

For many years, so-called higher critics assured student pastors in liberal seminaries that Moses could not possibly have written the first five books of the Bible. Why? They said there was no such thing as the writing of anything at the time of Moses. End of discussion.

Then the written laws of the Babylonian King Hammurabi were discovered. To the consternation of the "higher critics," these detailed laws proved to have been written three hundred years before Moses lived.

Critics have sniped at every detail in the Bible, no matter how minute, to try to prove it unreliable. In his book *Archaeology of Palestine*, noted archaeologist William F. Albright, writes: "Discovery after discovery has established the accuracy of innumerable details, and has brought increased recognition of the value of the Bible as a source of history."

Some historians have denied the existence of Jesus as a historical figure. They say, "We cannot accept the Bible's word that Jesus lived." If you should encounter an unbeliever who asks you, "How can you be sure that Jesus ever lived?" you can assure that person that no qualified historian would consider Jesus a myth. Even excluding the Bible, there is far more evidence that Jesus lived than there is for the existence of Shakespeare.

Many who need help, but who do not know who Jesus is, see no verification that God has ever done anything to help them. They see no evidence that anyone in the world can help them, or that anyone even cares. Such an outlook becomes fertile ground for fear.

Your fear may be different. You may nourish a hope that God has been with you, yet remember times when He didn't answer your prayers. You may feel as though you have been knocked about by life; if something bad could happen, it did. Murphy's Law seemed to be in full force!

You may doubt that you have been good enough for God to intervene in your life, or that you ever will be. This gives you ample reason to face the future with fear.

Why Doesn't God Help Me? you cry.

Why doesn't God solve our problems right away when we sincerely seek His help? A vision I had helped me to answer this question.

I saw a pool table with multicolored balls scattered about. However, one was different. It had the letter M printed all over it. This ball had to get to a white spot on the table for the game to end.

The cue stick hit the M ball and sent it crashing into the other balls, which then scattered back and forth across the table. The M ball was bounced back and forth by the movement of the others, stopping close to the white spot but never on it. Close was not good enough, and the game seemed endless. I thought, Why does this game go on and on? The M ball will never stop exactly on the tiny white spot. What can be the purpose of all this?

None of it made sense. I was sorely tempted to pick up the ball and place it on the white spot myself. As my hand moved to do so, the entire scene disappeared.

As I thought about what I had seen, I began to understand. The M ball was for me – Merlin. As in the game, there is an exact spot at which God wants me to be. He has used many forces to influence my life. Although I didn't see His hand, He caused or permitted many experiences to move me from one situation to another. He touched the life of one person, who in turn touched someone else, who in turn would touch my life. Now I'm sure that He has always been involved in every detail of my life.

Sometimes I've felt like shouting, "What's the point of my being knocked back and forth all over the place, when You could easily put me exactly where You want me to be?"

Some of my experiences have been delightful, others miserable. But every one of them had the same purpose: to get me where I needed to be. Viewed with this perspective, the misfortunes in my past are no longer painful memories.

When you feel manipulated by experiences that make no sense to you, picture the pool table I mentioned, and see your name on one of the balls. Don't be dismayed by the ugly things that people may say or do to you. People and circumstances may be able to move you from one place to another, but they cannot control your reactions. Only you can do that. If you decide to be angry, resentful, or bitter, it may be a long time before God moves you to the place you need to be.

Once we learn to trust God, He will use whatever people do for us – or against us – to move us to His chosen place. If we need to be embarrassed, He will send someone to take care of that need. Remember the verse: *God shall supply all your need according to His riches in glory by Christ Jesus* (Phil. 4:19). God always causes those things to happen that will meet our needs. After all, He holds the cue stick.

God sees the sparrow that falls. He numbers the hairs on our heads. Nothing – absolutely nothing – can happen without His knowledge. Our faith in His absolute control over all things defeats all kinds of fear.

Steve Largent, a football player with the Seattle Seahawks, put it this way: "I thank God I never had it easy. He's the One who built that obstacle course, who set up the hurdles, in order for me to grow."

Steve faced many obstacles, yet continued to do his best. His high school coach told him that he was too small and too slow to excel at football. But Steve loved football, so he kept working, kept improving his skills.

When Steve sought college scholarships, he was told the same thing time after time: he was too small, too slow. But Steve kept working and believing that God would help him over the seemingly insurmountable obstacles. Finally, Tulsa University awarded him a scholarship. In his junior and senior years he led the nation in touchdown catches.

Are you backed into a corner with some problem? Do you feel alone and helpless? Jesus promised, *Lo, I am with you always, even to the end of the age* (Matt. 28:20).

Fear tries to discourage us, whispering, "You are alone and helpless." Faith, however, comforts us, assuring, "God is with me!"

Chapter 10

Unfair Predicaments

I felt a wonderful surge of relief when I first accepted the fact that I would never be perfect.

We can be easily irritated when people find fault with us. Most of us have a craving to be perfect and to have our perfection recognized and praised. But we are not perfect, and we never will be.

We need not feel hurt when people point out our imperfections. Instead, we can find ways to make their opinions work for our good. By doing so, we are bound to profit regardless of what people say about us.

Understanding my imperfections made it much easier for me to accept the negative things people said about me. A heavy burden rolled off my shoulders. I came to understand why Paul wrote so freely about his imperfections. He wrote, *Christ Jesus came into the world to save sinners, of whom I am chief* (1 Tim. 1:15).

We are distracted from what God thinks of us if other people's opinions upset us. God is pleased when we can bear the derogatory opinions of others with the confidence that He will work them for our good. We can often profit from constructive criticism, of course, but it is God's opinion of us that should be at the very center of our concerns.

We often respond to criticism in such a negative way that we cannot profit from it. But if we value *God's* opinion rather that those of our detractors, He will cause their criticism to benefit us, no matter how severe it may be. This God-focused approach will make our lives so much easier to live.

During my lifetime I seemed to be backed into many corners with no way out, no relief in sight, no one to help. I felt utterly helpless, yet help did come. As I look back on those experiences, one factor stands out: each time I learned something new. Each caused me to become stronger and grow in the realization that Someone was on my side, someone who watched for the right moment to come to my aid.

During some of my most difficult experiences it seemed that God had allowed me to be pushed into unfair predicaments.

Once my wife Mary was seriously ill and in horrendous pain. We cried out to God for a healing miracle. He had healed us of other infirmities, but this time our prayers and those of hundreds of other loving people produced nothing – or so we thought. Mary's condition worsened. She became so ill that she couldn't dress, wash herself, sit, stand up, or even lie in bed without severe pain. My fears escalated.

Then the Lord asked me a question that posed an agonizing dilemma: If He would answer only one prayer, what would it be? Would I ask Him to heal Mary, or would I ask Him to help us get permission to distribute 250,000 copies of a condensed version of *Prison to Praise*? What a question! For months we had pleaded with the publisher to give us permission to do the printing. I knew that such a massive distribution could lead many people to Christ and eternal life. But more than anything I could ask for myself, I desperately wanted Mary to be healed. Her suffering tortured me.

In my agony I made my decision, I asked God to help us get permission to print the 250,000 copies of *Prison to Praise*. We got the permission, printed them, and sent copies to the darkest corners of the world.

That was many years ago, yet to this day we still receive word that people are accepting Jesus as they read this book.

Mary continued to hurt, and I died inside as I watched her suffer. Her pain spread to nearly every movable joint in her body. The specialist shook his head and predicted a lifetime of pain and confinement to a wheelchair. If she had taken the strongest medications available, they would have given her only partial relief. How Satan must have smiled!

Some people hinted that some secret sin must lurk in Mary's life. How God must have grieved. I certainly did.

We sought help in Mexico, read dozens of books, and explored other possible remedies. Our confidence in God was pushed to the limit. At times our emotions alternated between faith and fear, but we held fast: "God, You will help us. You will! We praise You through our tears. You are working this for our good."

Finally He answered! Not with a miracle healing, but with a natural remedy that eventually removed 95 percent of Mary's pain. The remedy to which He led us is not for everyone. It probably would be ineffective for many people with the same problem. What is important is that God led us to the solution that was right for us. There are vital lessons that we all must learn along our way. Often the journey itself is more important than the destination.

Not only did we print the 250,000 copies *Prison to Praise*, but something else happened that was beyond our expectations – something we had never dreamed of asking God to do.

California Bound

On our cross-country trek to California in 1972, Mary and I had the wonderful opportunity to spend several days with friends in Moran, Wyoming. There we met Pete and Gretchen Finch. Gretchen arranged for a praise meeting to be held in their home. Pete admitted to me later that he had not been happy about having a preacher in his home.

That meeting was one of those memorable, extra-special times. As a result, Pete later received Jesus as his Savior, and became an enthusiastic student of the Bible. And eventually he pastored his own church.

Years later I conducted meetings in that area, and stayed with the Finches. Pete took me on a horseback ride into the magnificent Grand Teton mountains around Moran and Jackson Hole. Those mountains reach high into the sky, and the valleys are treasure lands of beauty. A deep feeling of peace and reverence warmed my heart as I surveyed God's wondrous creation.

While enjoying our friends' hospitality, I became acquainted with an attorney who also was a guest. As I reluctantly prepared to leave for home, he said, "Merlin, my office is in New Jersey. If you ever need legal help in that part of the country, please call me." Legal help in New Jersey? Why would I ever need that? Yet I would learn that God often brings people and events into our lives that at the time seem of little significance.

Sometime after we had printed the special edition of *Prison to Praise*, I received some bad news. The publisher of my books had declared bankruptcy. The printing of our books would stop, with legal proceedings that could go on for months – or years. Would the message of praise to God be put on hold for that long? How could *that* possibly be a part of His plan?

One day as I worked at thanking the Lord for the new problem, the remark of the New Jersey attorney flashed into my mind. The publishing firm was also in New Jersey! Looking through my notes for his number, I wondered if he was still there. He was. He promised to look into the matter, and soon he called back.

"Merlin, I have good news. We can do better than getting permission for you to print your books. I believe we can get the publishing rights back in your name." Back in my name? I had no idea such a thing could be done. In a few days the attorney called to ask if I could come to New Jersey to meet with the attorney named by the court as trustee. We could talk in court during the bankruptcy hearings. You can imagine how quickly I said, "Yes!"

We met with the trustee during a court recess. In a few minutes the trustee was back in court addressing the judge: "Your honor, I recommend that the publishing rights for the books by Merlin R. Carothers be given to him."

"So ordered."

"What do we do next?" I asked the trustee.

"Nothing. It's all done. The books are yours. You can do whatever you want with them."

My vision had been only big enough to ask God to help us get permission to print a special edition of only one book. God, however, had made it possible to continue printing *all* of the praise books.

Our entire ministry was revolutionized. Previously we had paid the publisher twice the printing cost for the books we donated to people in the service, hospital patients, and prisoners. Now we could print hundreds of thousands of copies at the lowest rates available.

My faith took a giant leap forward. Millions of people could be reached! My lifelong vision of evangelizing the world, one at a time or by the millions, was a step closer. And I was one step closer to understanding why God wants us to be delivered from fear.

Reaching the World

What prevents millions of people from becoming Christians today? Is it greed, lust, pleasure, indifference – or what? What would cause millions of men and women to make personal decisions to forsake all and follow Christ this year? More churches? More Bibles? More Christian television and books? More dedicated pastors? Great catastrophes? Or would it require multiple, clearly irrefutable miracles?

The answer is simple: none of the above!

God sent His Son to the earth with His plan of salvation. Jesus gave us the formula, but something has gone terribly amiss: *Fear* prevents the good news of salvation by faith in Jesus from being shared with every person in our nation and the world. Let me emphasize the word *fear*.

Our greatest need is not for more finances, expensive tools, or more classes on how to evangelize. I took courses in college and seminary that taught evangelical techniques, and I have read many well-written books on the subject. I've conducted many classes and inspired thousands of Christians to go out into their communities with the message that had brought each of them eternal life. These things are useful, but knowing what to say or how to say it will never cause any of us to overcome our fears.

Fear can bind us as powerfully as the strongest chairs. It can destroy communication as effectively as cutting out the tongue. Fear paralyzes the following:

- Good intentions
- Enthusiasm
- Determination
- Zeal and passion to tell others about our Savior

Shakespeare wrote, "Our fears do make us traitors."

After Jesus was arrested, Peter had a prime opportunity to tell others about Him. But he was so intimidated that he cursed and swore he didn't know Him.

I'm thankful that Peter failed so miserably. His surrender to fear gives us a clear picture of what we all will do if we allow fear to control us. We may not curse and swear that we don't know our Savior, but we may act as if we don't.

Please remember this: Jesus is as alive today as He was when Peter denied knowing Him. He sees what we do when we have opportunities to tell others that He is our friend.

We leave a part of ourselves wherever we go, and wherever we go God gives us the incredible ability to influence the eternal destinies of our fellow human beings.

Take a walk down a street, across a road, and into a forest where you follow no pathway. Walk for five, ten, or twenty miles, being careful to leave no trail. Leave no evidence that you have passed that way.

Twenty-four hours later a well-trained dog can follow your trail. How? Not by sight, for you left no visible trail. The dog puts his nose to the ground and sniffs the scent you left there and in the air. He smells not only your shoes, but also your distinctive scent that went through them and into the ground. You weren't aware of leaving anything behind, but you did.

Lukewarm believers carry with them the scent of fear. Bold believers, however, speak up, witness, leave their mark – not the scent of fear!

In Jesus' parable of the talents (Matt. 25 TLB), one servant was given $5,000, another $2,000, the third $1,000. The man who received the $1,000 hid it in the ground. He doubted his ability to use it, so never even tried.

If you justify hiding your talents because you think of yourself as untalented, Jesus says to you, *The man who uses well what he is given shall be given more, and he shall have abundance. But from the man who is unfaithful, even what little responsibility he has shall be taken from him* (Matt. 25:29 TLB).

I've encouraged many people to use the simple talent of speaking to others by telephone. Help to organize a survey through your church. Then call people listed in your local telephone book. Introduce yourself in whatever way seems comfortable to you. You might say, "I'm a member of the XYZ church, and I'm making a survey. I'm not asking you to attend our church. I just want your opinion. What do you think a person needs to do in order to go to heaven?"

Then, if you discover that that person has not heard the good news of the gospel, you can share it with him. Some folks are using this method so successfully that they are leading an average of one person to Christ every day!

Now let's consider what makes a church.

Chapter 11

What Makes a Church?

Fear should never cause us to allow others with many or great talents to do all the work of sharing the good news. Here is a sequence that is too often repeated:

Two bold, courageous Christians meet and discuss their mutual desire to bring men and women to Christ. They bring two others to Him.

Now, four unafraid, zealous Christians go out and win four others. Soon they are eight, sixteen, thirty-two, and sixty-four in number.

One man becomes the pastor. A beautiful church building is erected and dedicated to bringing men and women to Christ. The pastor is declared responsible for keeping the church organized. During the week, he meets with many leaders from within its fold.

The choir director stresses the need for new choir members and urges the pastor to mention this "next Sunday." The Sunday school superintendent urges the pastor to plead for teachers "next Sunday." The youth director pleads for him to urge members to help with the youth activities "next Sunday."

The most emotional plea of all comes from the treasurer. He warns the pastor that unless he inspires people to give more, the budget in every department in the church must be cut. This is not good news. Everyone is *afraid* that something must be done.

When the pastor steps to the pulpit Sunday morning, his mind is crammed with all the programs he must push. He thinks, What if I fail? Everything must be squeezed into the one hour allotted to him by his sheep. To cut any of the sacred moments given to the choir or music director would be unthinkable. Neither can he shortchange any special projects. And if the people don't give their tithes, the entire church will collapse.

So he urges the congregation to contribute to all these good and important projects. The church supports itself. Some mention is made of the need to reach the unsaved, but that isn't the heart and soul of the church. The pastor, his assistants, the elders, and the heads of each department have as their first priority its preservation.

The church may temporarily increase in attendance. Its people will doubtless appreciate its youth programs, nursery, well-organized Sunday school, choir, and inspiring sermons. But the people have stopped witnessing for Christ, and soon become afraid to do so.

If this scenario were typical of only one church in a community, the results would not be fatal. But when many churches become centered only on supporting themselves, the spirit of evangelism gradually dies. They become places to meet and eat, mere social clubs. Winning people to Christ and taking care of them are inseparable, but each must be kept in balance if the church is to reach its divine objective.

My own denomination, Methodism, was once a flaming fire of evangelism. Converts were trained to go out and win others to Christ. People who had a passion for reaching the lost were placed in charge of others who wanted to reach them. Anyone who feared being beaten, stoned, or put into prison was never appointed as a teacher or preacher. Their enthusiasm and refusal to be afraid caused Methodists to reach across

England, Colonial America and, ultimately, the world. These ardent evangelists met in fields, forests, and brush arbors. They were exhorted to share the good news of the gospel with everyone in the world.

Their leader, John Wesley, did not intend to start a denomination. His burning passion was centered exclusively on winning souls to Christ. Wesley frequently walked straight toward raging mobs screaming that he should be killed. This fiery 110-pound giant became characterized as the man who knew no fear.

Wesley's fearless stance caused him to become my hero. I've remembered his fearlessness when I've faced fearsome situations of my own.

When I was assigned as pastor of a Methodist circuit in 1948, one of the churches looked terrible. It's exterior had been neglected for so long that its paint was barely visible. When I asked why it hadn't been painted, I was told, "There are two factions in the church. They can never agree on how the necessary money is to be raised, and so nothing is ever done."

In one faction was a man who was known as the financial pillar of the church. Many people looked to him to take care of most of the church's financial needs. Because of this the people were always afraid of his being offended. The other faction, somewhat smaller, resented this man's control over everything in the church, so they refused to cooperate with anything he wanted done.

I went to visit the "financial pillar." When I arrived at his farm, he was in the barn shoveling manure with a pitchfork. During our conversation he told me what he thought should be done to raise the money to paint the church. I replied, "No, that's not what I am going to do." That was not what he expected to hear from a young, new preacher. He stopped his work, thrust his pitchfork toward me, and walked straight at me.

He shouted, "Yes, you will, or you're finished!" I stood my ground, focusing on his eyes. He was furious, fire and brimstone stoking his rage. This man, I had heard, was used to ministers doing whatever he said. If they didn't, he would take whatever actions he considered appropriate.

I had abundant reason to be afraid. This man was obviously unpredictable, and I was barely beginning my long journey from fear to faith. As I stood my ground, I remembered John Wesley. His courage inspired me. I moved toward the enraged man, but I couldn't go far because the prongs of the pitchfork were poised perilously close to my throat. The next few minutes seemed to last forever, but finally he saw that I wasn't going to back down. You may be sure that I was relieved when he lowered the pitchfork, told me to leave, turned his back, and went back to work.

The next Sunday I told the congregation the decision I had made regarding the painting of the church: "Raising funds will not be necessary," I said. "I'll be here ready to work next Saturday morning at 6:00 a.m. with a bucket of paint. Anyone who wants to help, please bring your paintbrush."

One man spoke up, "But what about the steeple? You can't paint it. It's too high. We need professionals for that." And it *was* high.

"I'll paint it" I replied boldly, although I had never before painted even a building, let alone a church steeple. All that week I was tempted to worry about the steeple that seemed to reach into the heavens.

Saturday morning came and, to my immense delight twelve men showed up to help their young, bold preacher. But before they began, they wanted to see how I intended to paint the steeple that was obviously too high for any ladder to reach.

"Lord, what do I do now?" Then an image entered

my mind. I had been trained by the Army to blow up bridges. That's it! I thought. God had arranged for me to attend Demolitions School so that years later I could paint a church steeple! Isn't God clever? Soon I had ropes rigged over the steeple from which I could hang to paint.

From then on I was a hero to nearly every man in the church. They started bringing new men to see their "daring and resourceful preacher." Soon money poured in to pay for everything we needed, and then some. Attendance increased and soon doubled.

The church lost its financial pillar, of course, but members didn't seem to mind. Fear takes a back seat when faith controls our actions.

Evangelical Fervor

Fear caused the original evangelical fervor of Christians in our country to be replaced by a "survival mentality." This attitude causes us to lose sight of our primary mission: saving souls. When church members do not birth new Christians, stagnation and decay set in.

Have you ever seen a woman's eyes light up when she sees someone else's baby? She wants to hold it and gaze at it in rapt attention. Often her first thought is, I want a baby! The sight of that mother and child causes her to want to bear her own child.

The enthusiasm of new converts inspires other Christians. They want to go out and birth converts of their own. Victories beget new victories.

My enthusiasm increases as I realize what can happen if Christians regain their potential to influence the people of the world. You may be a young person with no experience or training, or a mature adult with much experience and many talents. You may be an older citizen on a fixed income, or a successful executive. You may enjoy nearly perfect health, or use a wheelchair. Whatever your status or condition in life, you have unlimited potential to persuade others to receive Jesus as their Lord and Savior. You and I have the exalted opportunity to allow God to speak through us. We have only one problem: If we are afraid, God will find someone else to do His work.

Jesus urged His followers to "Tell the good news to every nation and to every person." If every believer in the world would lead one person to Christ each year (not one per day or one per month, just one per year), how long do you think it would take to win the world to Him? Not very long.

The World Christian Encyclopedia indicates that there are now more than 1.5 billion Christians in the world today. What if just 3 percent of them could be delivered from the terrible shackles of fear, enabling them to spend a few minutes a day telling unbelievers the good news? That would amount to 50 million dedicated, active Christians. If each of these birthed yet another active Christian, next year there would be 100 million. The results would continue as follows:

2d year—200 million
3d year—400 million
4th year—800 million
5th year—I billion, 600 million
6th year—3 billion, 200 million
7th year—6 billion, 400 million

Satan is well aware of this potential. He heard Jesus say, "Preach the gospel to every creature." He knows his time is short and that he must silence the mouths of believers.

Jesus spent His final moments here on earth urging us to go and tell all the world the good news. He will return when all is ready. What is the exact date of His return? Read on, and I'll tell you.

What is Christ's plan? Romans 11:25 provides the clearest answer that I see in the entire Bible: *Israel has experienced a hardening in part until the full number of the Gentiles has come in*.

What a challenge! What a reason to build God's kingdom with every ounce of our strength! Jesus will descend from heaven when the full number of gentiles is complete! To me, that means He waits for us to complete our assignment and, once we do, He will claim His throne here on Earth. He will end war, suffering, pain, and fear. But first we must complete our assignment.

On Trial

The court is in session and the trial in progress. All attention is focused on the witness. The judge, jury, prosecuting and defense attorneys, bailiff, and court and news reporters wait expectantly. Everyone wants to know, "What will the witness say? Will he verify the prosecuting attorney's claims or those of the defendant?"

For now, the witness is the center of attention. The outcome of the trial depends on what he says.

He is silent. Everyone leans forward in anticipation of what he may say. He remains silent.

The judge becomes impatient. "Answer the question, please."

Still the witness says nothing. Reporters poise their pencils. The jury stirs impatiently, wondering why the witness hasn't spoken.

Finally the judge says, "Sir, either you must answer the question, or I must hold you in contempt."

And so it is. A witness who is too afraid to speak can

be held in contempt. God asks us, *And how can they hear about Him unless someone tells them?* (Rom. 10:14 TLB). If only 10 percent of the readers of this book were to cast off their shackles of fear, they could bring hundreds of millions of people to Christ.

The vast country of Russia was brought under communist control by fewer than 10 percent of its people. That 10 percent then brought billions of other people under the ruthless control of atheism. Here in the United States, the agendas of both major political parties are controlled by only 10 percent of their respective members. Ten percent of all Christians, then, could launch a spiritual awakening that could set the wold afire for Christ!

You may be tempted to think, *But I'm just one person. There is little that I can do to change the world.* Most of us will never have the opportunity to speak to millions of people, but when we tell even one person about our faith in God, His power is behind us. Our mouths speak the words that carry the strength of His power.

Here is a disturbing estimate: About 95 percent of unbelievers in the United States have never heard the good news that they can receive the free gift of eternal life simply by inviting Jesus to be their Lord and Savior. Why? The good news is preached in churches, where few unbelievers go, on Christian television programs that unbelievers seldom watch, and in books that unbelievers can ignore if they choose. Unbelievers have little cause to be concerned with the good news we are reporting. They rarely or never hear it.

Jesus defeated Satan's master plan to hold the entire human race in slavery. Then He placed the completion of His plan in our hands. What a magnificent calling we have!

Olympic Contenders

Fear, even in the minutest proportion, can defeat the loftiest ambitions. After an Olympics competition, I listened to interviews with gold medallists. Contestants were asked if they expected to win. The winners always answered "yes!" They always *expected* to win. The contenders said their attitudes had to be perfect when they stepped up to the starting line. Even one negative feeling could destroy a lifetime of arduous preparation. They could think no negative thoughts whatsoever. None!

You may think, How is it possible not to think a thought if that thought enters your mind? Olympic contenders, though, must learn to control the thoughts that enter their minds, or they don't win.

Paul said that we are in a race, and that we are to run that race as if we expect to win it. If fear enters our minds, we will fail. Other people may then have to pay the price for our failures. They may miss the gift of eternal life. We then forfeit the reward of our Father saying, *Well done, good and faithful servant* (Matt. 25:21).

The church is the army of the Lord. Armies often are destroyed because the soldiers are afraid. The annals of warfare, in fact, are filled with accounts of entire armies put to flight not by the enemy, but by fear. If one man in the front ranks turns and flees in panic, he can cause every soldier behind him to flee in panic with him. What was once an army becomes an undisciplined horde.

From the first day a man enters military service the main order of business is to teach him discipline. Every drill and marching order is designed to instill rigid conformity. Each soldier must put his left foot forward in exact unison with his ninety-nine comrades. Each must start, turn, reverse direction, run, or stop, all in harmony with the rest. Every minute of every day he is trained to respond only to orders. After many months of such discipline he begins to respond to every command as though it were his own idea. Stubborn vestiges of fear may still lurk within him, but rigorous discipline, consistently imposed, increases the likelihood that he will respond in a disciplined manner.

God calls on us to live a disciplined life: *We are to bring every thought into captivity to the obedience of Christ* (2 Cor. 10:5).

Chapter 12

A Nugget of Pure Gold

For more than fifty-three years I have written and talked about faith. Now, at age seventy-six, I have a clearer understanding of how faith should work in everyday life. I will rejoice if I can help you to understand what I have learned.

I wasn't thinking about Abraham, but the thought came to me: *Abraham believed God, and it was accounted to him for righteousness* (Rom. 4:3).

A question formed in my mind: What did Abraham do that caused God to credit him with righteousness? My answer was, He believed God.

Then came the question, How long did Abraham believe God? The answer: for many years.

Keep thinking about that.

As I meditated, a light suddenly turned on in my mind. Something important – really important – had been revealed to me.

Abraham was seventy-five years old when God told him to leave his friends and family in Haran and travel to a strange country. Not knowing where he was going, or why, he headed south toward the land of the Canaanites, on to Egypt, then back up to the land of Canaan. This trek extended to more than one thousand miles. It was, indeed, a journey of faith.

Travel, Abraham style, involved walking with his wife and all his goats, sheep, cattle and donkeys. The animals, it can be supposed, moved at their own pace and insisted on grazing nearly every step of the way. The going was slow and tedious.

Abraham and his family carried their tents and set up camp at the end of each day's hot and dusty trek. They spread their blankets by the light of the campfire and settled down to sleep on the floor of a strange desert. Upon awakening the next morning there was more of the same – more trudging toward an unknown destination over land they had never seen until God gave them some signal that it was time to stop. Would there be adequate food and water? What fearsome enemies lurked out there waiting to attack and kill? For how many days could they trudge onward without knowing where they were or where they were going? But Abraham refused to turn back. Each day, perhaps every hour, he had to renew his decision to walk by faith.

When Abraham was one hundred years old and Sarah ninety, God rewarded their walk of faith. Up to that time they had no children, although He had promised them that their descendants would be as numerous as the stars.

Some years after Isaac was born, Abraham faced an even greater test of his faith. God told him to kill his beloved son. Yet Abraham continued to believe that God would keep His promise.

As I meditated on Abraham's unwavering faith, the Holy Spirit opened my understanding. Before this experience, I had always believed there was something wrong with my faith if I prayed and nothing happened. Have you done the same? I felt that God must be displeased with me, though I didn't know why.

When a Scripture verse, sermon, or someone's testimony stimulated my faith, I would try again to believe that God had answered my prayer. If nothing "worthwhile" happened, I would again become discouraged. Does this sound familiar?

I was most tempted to become discouraged and

give up when I prayed for physical healing. In desperation I would pray, fast, and study Bible verses on faith. Then I would try to stretch my faith as far as it would go. If nothing happened immediately, I would slide back into a feeling of defeat.

As we have seen, however, Abraham didn't pray and believe that way. He persisted – he *kept on believing*. As the years passed he continued to believe God, regardless of his circumstances. As a result, his faith became the cornerstone of God's message to all generations.

James 2:23 describes the high position that God gave to Abraham: *Abraham was called the friend of God*. We, too, should eagerly grasp every opportunity to be *God's friend*. He gives us the opportunity to do so every time we face a difficult circumstance.

Have you ever wondered why a family has a child who suffers from serious disabilities? God didn't cause this heartache, but He did allow it. Such suffering often wraps these families with a special bond of love that other families never experience. God permits these families to be thrust into such a painful and difficult role so that their faith can stretch. Every day they are challenged to believe that He is working something for their good. Throughout eternity they, too, may be honored by God for the righteousness they earned by their persistent faith. They, too, may earn the incomparable distinction of being among "God's friends."

At times, prayer may seem like a journey into unknown territory. We know we should pray, but may be tempted to wonder, *Is this really doing any good*?

As I pondered over Abraham's journey of faith, thoughts of my old restlessness during prayer came to mind. I recalled the dozens of times my prayers had been interrupted by anxious thoughts about the many "important" things I had to do that day. At the conclusion of those times of prayer I wondered if the time had been well spent, or if I should have used it in serving the Lord in some more tangible way.

Our carnal minds are crafty in their ability to make decisions that may *seem* right, but end up being more favorable to the flesh than to the spirit. For example, we can tell ourselves, "I will show real faith in God. I will proclaim each morning, 'Lord, I trust You to meet all of my needs today. To prove my faith in You I will not bother You again today. Amen.'" Then, satisfied that we are "trusting God," we can go about our business.

Prayer may at first be the simple declaration: "God, I know You are there, and I will keep talking to You." This is important, for every moment we talk with Him we are showing our faith!

At other times, our prayers should manifest intense zeal. Luke 22:44 describes Jesus' intense zeal: *And being in agony, He prayed more earnestly. Then His sweat became like great drops of blood falling down to the ground.*

Men of the Old Testament often prayed with intensity. For example, Moses said, *And I fell down before the Lord, as at the first, forty days and forty nights; I neither ate bread nor drank water, because of all your sin which you committed in doing wickedly in the sight of the Lord, to provoke Him to anger* (Deut. 9:18). Moses believed that God was listening to him, so he kept praying until he received an answer.

James 5:17 tells us: *Elijah was a man with a nature like ours, and he prayed earnestly that it would not rain; and it did not rain on the land for three years and six months.*

God didn't design prayer to be a form of punishment, although I sometimes felt that it was. Rather, prayer is our perfect opportunity to learn how to enter His presence. *Prayer is faith in action*!

A Measure of Faith

Throughout the Bible there are many illustrations of what happens when people learn to believe God. Do you believe what the Bible says about faith? I don't mean, "Do you understand it?" You don't have to understand faith to believe in its power.

We know that each of us does have faith: G*od has dealt to each one a measure of faith* (Rom. 12:3). We must learn how to use what we have.

Positive thinking says, "I can do all things." This attitude, however, eventually leads to a brick wall. Faith in Christ says, *I can do all things through Christ who strengthens me* (Phil. 4:13).

A man at Lystra had never walked. He heard Paul speak, paid attention, believed God, and did what Paul told him to do. Paul said, *'Stand up!' The man leaped to his feet and started to walk* (Acts 14:8–10).

Another man, who had never before walked, asked Peter for money. Peter answered him, *In the name of Jesus Christ of Nazareth, rise up and walk. In an instant the man's feet and anklebones were healed* (Acts 3:1-10).

You might think that if Peter or Paul were here to help me, I could then believe. But they aren't here, which is why God preserved their words so we could read them and learn. Their words cry, "Stand up! Don't wait for someone else's faith to help you. Use the faith you have!"

I challenge you to use your faith in such a simple way that you may wonder why you never thought of it. You may have felt unable to believe that you were 100 percent free from sickness or some other physical problem. You may have felt that no matter how hard you tried you still suffered.

Peter and Paul didn't ask suffering people to "feel better." They commanded them to stand up and walk. I'm not asking *you* to feel better, because feelings often cannot be trusted. I'm suggesting that you take a completely different route.

Believe whatever you can believe. Believe that today you have twice as much joy as you did yesterday. Believe that today you can be a better person than you were yesterday. You can do it! Ignore what your mind naturally wants to feel. Look instead at what you believe is God's gift to you through Christ who came to give us His righteousness.

Reach out in faith as far as you can go. Believe that you are stronger – even twice as strong – as you were before. That will be using the "measure of faith" that God has given you.

When I practice using the small measure of faith that I have, I feel a new surge of strength, a new certainty that this is exactly what God promised to all His children. Those who hope in the Lord will:

- renew their strength.
- soar on wings like eagles.
- run and not grow weary.
- walk and not faint (see Isa. 40:31).

When I allow myself to become distressed by the turmoil of a hectic day, nothing seems to go right. But when I believe God is using that day to bless me and complete His plan for me, my strength and joy leap upward.

Sometimes I feel tired and discouraged. I just want to relax under a shade tree and ignore all my responsibilities. But if I give in to these feelings, eventually I will become like a tree that bears no fruit, a tree that

God will cut down. God wants us to be excited about the opportunity He gives us to *fight the good fight of faith* (1 Tim. 6:12).

When the problems of life begin to bear down on you, don't give in to feelings of discouragement or despair. Claim your God-given rights.

Jesus Was Excited

Consider the enormous potential that we have to cause every event, of every day, to create joy in us. Even stress, strain, and past fears can be forced to bring us new happiness.

Jesus often spoke in parables that were difficult to understand. When asked why He did so, He explained that some people were not ready to understand. I too, have only recently begun to understand the essence of John 7:38: *He who believes in Me, as the Scripture has said, out of his heart will flow rivers of living water.* Like most people, my main interest often has been the pursuit of fun, entertainment, and from things outside myself. My understanding of the power of this Scripture was limited.

While attending a special feast, *Jesus stood and cried out, saying, 'If anyone thirsts, let him come to Me and drink'* (John 7:37). Jesus was obviously excited as He uttered these words. He knew we could receive something from Him that would be like living water flowing out of us. His offer still stands to those who persist in their eagerness to understand Him.

The Bible uses a form of the word joy 201 times. Joy is a major part of the Christian gospel, yet too often it occupies only a small place in Christian living. Everyone wants joy, but most folks don't know how to revel in it. Most people seek only temporary happiness, and that is a poor substitute for the joy that caused Jesus to be so excited.

The inner joy that wells up like a fountain within us, never depends on our circumstances or what others say or do to us. Think of that. What a relief! What a way to live!

In Philippians 4:7, Paul wrote about something that lived within him. He called it *the peace of God, that passes all understanding*. Imagine a peace the passes all understanding! You can't, of course, so don't despair if you don't understand. You must, however, persist in learning how to live in it.

Remember. Our circumstances should never control our joy. Understand this, and life takes on a completely new quality and meaning.

In Acts 13:52 (Amplified), we learn that *the disciples were continually filled [throughout their souls] with joy and the Holy Spirit*. It is faith that creates joy, and joy is God's objective for you and me.

It's tragic that so many Christians feel that God has deserted them if they aren't healthy, prosperous, popular, and loved by spouses, children and friends. But they can still be numbered among God's most treasured children even if they lack all these blessings. You can too.

I'm serious. It's true! Don't punish yourself when people point out and criticize you because of the difficulties you endure. They may mean well, but they are dead wrong. Nearly every person in the Bible had severe problems. Even so, they were the people God used.

Be a joyful child of God and: *Shout to God with the voice of triumph!* (Ps. 47:1). No matter what is happening to you, declare your victory – to God, to yourself, and to those around you. Be assured that God will honor your declaration.

Psalm 37:4 says, *Delight yourself also in the Lord,*

and He shall give you the desires of your heart. What wonderful advice! Be delighted in whatever God permits to happen, and the rewards are unlimited. Job said, He will yet fill your mouth with laughing (Job 8:21). Romans 14:17 speaks of the "righteousness and peace and joy" of the kingdom of God. These verses, and many more, prove that God wants us to be joyful.

There may be situations in our daily lives that make us feel completely helpless – like there is nothing we can do. Such times as these can easily make us fearful and can challenge our faith. But when we realize that our circumstances, however severe, cannot diminish the joy of God within us, we are free – free indeed!

Every day I hear from men and women whose spouses have broken marriage vows or deserted them. Often they are bitterly angry and feel betrayed. Some are so devastated that they wish they could die. Does faith in God work in these situations, or should those who suffer merely give up and sink into a quagmire of fear?

Ready for the Unexpected

Certain painful experiences in my life have proven to me that my faith must be prepared for the unexpected. In 1952 I awakened in a hospital bed surrounded by bars. As my mind struggled to function, my first thought was, Where am I?

I had no memory of being ill or even leaving home. My head throbbed so painfully that I could barely lift it from the pillow. When my eyes focused I saw that the pillow bore the name of a hospital in Chicago, Illinois. Chicago, Illinois! My home was hundreds of miles from Chicago! How did I get here? Nothing in my life had prepared me for the trauma of that moment.

My next thought was, How could I be somewhere

and not know where I am? I must be in a hospital for the insane! My heart began to beat so wildly that I feared it would push its way through my chest.

In a very weak voice I began to cry, "Help, where am I?" No one responded. "Help! Help! Help!" Still no response.

Was I afraid? Yes, I was *really* afraid! There is no macho, reserve strength for such moments as those. What I needed was an inner reserve of faith that would have calmed and reassured me during those moments.

Finally, after what seemed like an eternity, my childhood friend, Frank Wigton, walked into the room. He told me later that he had been with me all night as I slipped in and out of consciousness.

"Frank, where am I? What has happened to me? Why am I in this hospital for the insane? Why are these bars all around me?"

"You aren't insane, Merlin. You were in an automobile accident while you were driving here to see me. You had my name and phone number with you, so the police called me last night after they brought you here. The bars are only to keep you from falling out of bed."

Frank lowered the bars on one side and held my hand. Tears still come to my eyes when I remember the peace that entered my heart as my dear friend grasped my hand. My fear, so acute, vanished in the presence of a friend who cared.

Since then I've learned the blessed reality of the peace that fills the troubled breast when we know that Jesus is holding our hands in even the most difficult situations: *I am with you always, even to the end of the age* (Matt. 28:20). What a glorious reality to live and abide in!

I learned later that my headache and memory loss had been caused by a concussion. After a short period of recovery I was able to leave the hospital. Even now, after nearly fifty years, I still have no memory of my drive to Chicago or the accident.

Since that day, I, too, have stood at the bedsides of many people who could not remember how they had ended up in the hospital. Some were the victims of accidents or war injuries. Others had suffered heart attacks or strokes. And I've ended up in the hospital with other severe problems. But since that fearful day so many years ago, I've learned how to keep building my faith so that should the unexpected happen, my faith will take over and destroy the fears that try to invade and control my thoughts.

Chapter 13

Steps of Faith

If we pray, "God, heal me," and there is no immediate change in our health, God hasn't forsaken us. He simply wants us to stand firm in our faith. Hebrews 11:37 speaks of those who were destitute, tormented, stoned – even put to the sword. Yet God looked upon them with favor. He considered their faith to be righteousness.

Some may ask, "What good does it do to have faith if I still have to suffer?" Paul answers this question by describing God's attitude toward those who believe: *God is not ashamed to be called their God* (Heb. 11:16).

Unbelievers demand deliverance now, not later. They want clear, convincing evidence that God is working before they will believe. Thomas, for example, said that until he saw the marks on Jesus' hands and feet, he would not believe He had been resurrected. To Thomas, that may have seemed like clear, rational thinking. But later Jesus said to him, *Thomas, because you have seen Me, you have believed. Blessed are those who have not seen and yet have believed* (John 20:29).

Mark 16:14 tells us: *He appeared to the eleven as they sat at the table; and He rebuked their unbelief and hardness of heart, because they did not believe those who had seen Him after He had risen*. Again Jesus said to them, *O foolish ones, and slow of heart to believe in all that the prophets have spoken!* (Luke 24:25).

All of us want to enter into the world of miracles, but few of us want to endure the day-by-day journeys in which we have to put one foot painfully in front of the other without knowing where we are going or why. We cannot enter a spiritual world that we don't understand until we learn to walk by faith in the world we do understand. Jesus said: *If I have told you earthly things and you do not believe, how will you believe if I tell you heavenly things?* (John 3:12).

Most of us think that it would be so much easier to have faith in God if only He would perform miracles for us. In John 4:48, however, Jesus rebuked: *Unless you people see signs and wonders, you will by no means believe*. Jesus was sorely distressed by those who refused to believe.

Where Is the Water?

Throughout the Old Testament God repeatedly blessed men and women who had the boldness to trust Him no matter how long they had to wait for the answers to their prayers. The story of Noah provides a case in point. Noah had no evidence that there would ever be a flood, yet he believed God and acted on what He told him to do.

For about one hundred years Noah and his three sons worked day after day to build a boat 450 feet long, 75 feet wide, and 45 feet high. These dimensions illustrate the enormity of the project that Noah faced. Not only would the boat be huge, but there was no water on which to float it once it was built. One hundred years of toil to build an enormous structure that ultimately might prove useless, required faith. Noah was the laughingstock of the land during those years, but in Hebrews 11:7, God honored him as the man who became *heir of the righteousness which is according to faith*.

During those one hundred long years (36,500 days), Noah might have asked himself thousands of times, "What good will all this work accomplish? Where is there enough water to float this monstrosity?" Nevertheless, he kept cutting trees and laboriously fashioning them into boards. How did he cut and shape them? There were few tools – certainly no steel or power tools – so he and his sons used crude stone axes of their own making. Now that is hard work! I wonder how many smashed fingers he had during those years? He had to cut the tree lengthwise. Talk about work! It might have taken days to make one board. Then he and his sons had to carry the huge and heavy boards to the building site.

Each board had to be precisely crafted to fit its position, then joined to other boards. Joined how? Noah had no nails, so he probably designed wooden ones. Finally, each seam had to be carefully water-proofed.

I emphasize these points because, like Noah's magnificent ark, our faith needs to be patterned, shaped, and defined by the word *persistence*. In fact, all the steps of faith have that same name – persistence.

Every day, perhaps every hour, Noah was required to reaffirm his faith that God would somehow use his labors to accomplish something. But what? I can imagine Noah saying, "Okay, God, You must have some good reason for all of this, so I'll keep working."

Noah's steadfastness caused him to be listed in God's Hall of Fame, and he became an example for us to follow. God listed him in the eleventh chapter of Hebrews as one of His heroes.

As I pondered Noah's story, my attitude toward many things changed. Each situation I encountered became a God-given opportunity for me to trust God. This, I saw, was the only way I could ever please Him. I repeat, *Without faith it is impossible to please [God]* (Heb. 11:6).

Jesus repeatedly encouraged us to have faith, and He promised us great rewards if we would learn. He said, *Did I not say to you that if you would believe you would see the glory of God?* (John 11:40); and *He who believes in Me, as the Scripture has said, out of his heart will flow rivers of living water* (John 7:38).

In Ephesians 1:19, Paul wrote about *the exceeding greatness of His power toward us who believe*. I've come to realize that during those times when my faith in God was weak, I spent little time in prayer. *Prayer*, after all, is *an expression of faith*, and if I have *little faith* I have *little incentive* to pray. Time spent in prayer is time saying, "God, I believe and trust in You." Sleepless nights can become a wonderful time to joyfully express our faith, as we talk to God!

God Is Making Me Well

What happens when we try our best to believe God, yet our faith is still weak? Consider the child whose father places her on a table and says, "Jump." I'll catch you." If the child is frightened, the father doesn't become angry. He simply moves a little closer and encourages the child again. The child then becomes more confident in her father and joyfully leaps into his arms.

As we continue to say, "Father, I trust You," our faith increases. We must keep taking steps of faith. For example, if we have a cold, it's easy to think, *I feel bad now and will probably feel even worse later on*. But if we think, I feel bad now, but God is making me well, our faith has an opportunity to grow.

When we trust Him, the Holy Spirit rewards us with joy and increased inner strength.

At times I hear the ugly voice of the god of this world. It whispers, "Merlin, you are sick and weary." If I listened to him, my day would be ruined. I would accomplish nothing worthwhile. So I say, "Enough of that! Be silent! I'm busy with God's work and will not listen to your lies!" Then my mind fills with trust as I begin to thank and praise God.

The following verse causes some people to be fearful and even to question their faith. If this verse is true, they think, then I must not be a Christian: *If you can believe, all things are possible to him who believes* (Mark 9:23).

Notice that Jesus said "if." This suggests to me that there will be times when we lack the faith to receive the things that we would like to have. What might cause us to be in this condition? John 15:16 gives us one answer: *Go and bear fruit, . . . that whatever you ask the Father in My name He may give you*. This makes me believe that we must bear fruit in order to receive *some* things from God. If there is some area of my life in which I do not want to do God's will, I may not be bearing the fruit that He requires of me. God requires different things from different people. He may require things from you that He would not ask of any other person.

Even in the most difficult circumstances Jesus refused to use His limitless power to help Himself. When He was on the cross, scoffers sneered, *Descend now from the cross, that we may see and believe* (Mark 15:32). But Jesus, obedient to God, died for us to save ourselves. We would have, instead, shown those scoffers a thing or two!

Over the years, God has helped me to learn many important principles regarding the joy and strength we receive when we praise Him for everything. I know that when I practice believing God, His power works in me. He continues to tell me, "Keep believing, son!"

We all have the same potential for belief that Abraham had. Consider Romans 3:22, which tells us how to believe. We, too, can gain membership in this elite group if we follow their example and believe.

More About Noah

Noah saw that the people around him were becoming increasingly evil and that wickedness prevailed everywhere. He fervently wanted to save his family from the evil around them, but what could he do? He was only one man, and those around him were not interested in what he had to say. God had told Noah, "A great flood of water is coming, so prepare."

"A flood? What is that?"

"Water will cover the whole earth so that everyone will die."

Noah might have said, "But, Lord, there isn't that much water anywhere. How can that possibly be?"

"Just believe Me, Noah, and do what I tell you. You are a righteous man, so you and your family will be spared."

Noah believed and set to work.

One man, Abraham, believed, and the nation of Israel was born. Out of Israel came Moses, and through him God's law was made known. Then came Jesus.

What will happen through you and me as we learn to believe God? Our potential is unlimited! God is still seeking men and women willing to believe Him and who will keep on believing Him regardless of what the evidence may seem to be.

Abraham didn't just believe – he *acted* on his belief. Day by day and one step at a time, he did what he thought God wanted him to do.

God has warned us that one day this world will be consumed by fire and that we, as believers, must build our "ark of safety." Our ark is formed by faith. Learning to believe is at least as difficult as building an ark, but we must persist. Noah had never seen an ark, but he believed God. He labored on, doing what God had commanded him.

You and I do not know how to believe God as completely as Jesus did, but we can still help our faith to grow. This requires commitment, but we must begin, and today is the best day we will ever have to begin. Starting today, let's believe that God is healing us and giving us all the strength and energy that we need. Let's believe that He is meeting all our needs and using us to prepare the way for the return of His Son. Starting right now, let's believe that He is giving us the ability to spread the Good News of the gospel to all the world!

God is still telling me, "Merlin, Abraham and Noah believed Me, and I count their belief as righteousness."

Chapter 14

Angels Among Us

I stood at the foot of my father's hospital bed. At twelve years of age it never occurred to me that he might never return home.

"Merlin, be a good boy." Those were his last words to me before someone ushered me out of the hospital room.

A short time later his heart stopped, and the attending physician gave him a shot to stimulate it. Mother told us later that Dad had opened his eyes and said, "That won't be necessary. I'm going now."

A few seconds later he raised himself to a sitting position and looked toward the foot of the bed. With a radiant smile on his face, he said, "Look, they've come for me!" Then he fell back and was gone.

I tell you this to share something that only recently came to my attention. My father's death was sixty-five years ago, yet it took all this time for the Holy Spirit to help me realize something of utmost importance.

The angels that my father saw at the foot of his bed were in the exact spot on which I had stood only minutes earlier. Why hadn't I seen or felt anyone there? Had those angels been at the foot of the bed when I had stood there?

Years later, when my father's mother lay awaiting death, another strange event happened. Grandmother motioned for me to come close, where she whispered in my ear, "Merlin, don't miss it!"

"Miss what, Grandmother?"

"The music! The music!"

She heard music, but I heard only her whispering. Why could she hear music, but I couldn't?

These are not isolated incidents. Thousands have heard people on the verge of death speak of things they could see and hear. Why do people near death often see and hear things that the rest of us do not?

For centuries, Christianity has taught us that God is omnipresent – everywhere. If so, He is right beside you right now. If He is there beside you, why can't you see or feel Him?

The Bible teaches us that there may be all kinds of things around us that we don't see:

And when the servant of the man of God arose early and went out, there was an army, surrounding the city with horses and chariots. And his servant said to him, *Alas, my master! What shall we do? So he answered, Do not fear, for those who are with us are more than those who are with them. And Elisha prayed, and said, Lord, I pray, open his eyes that he may see. Then the Lord opened the eyes of the young man, and he saw. And behold, the mountain was full of horses and chariots of fire all around Elisha* (2 Kings 6:15–17).

We, too, are probably surrounded by things we can't see or hear at this very moment.

Why don't we see and hear things in the spiritual realm around us? Were human beings always so oblivious to things not a part of the physical world? Are there things we could do that would open our eyes and ears to the unseen world?

The writers of the Old Testament did not explain how they were able to hear God speak to them, yet they heard and recorded page after page of His exact words. Jesus Himself quoted from the Old Testament often and confirmed that it contained God's words.

Do things still happen around us that we do not see?

Have you ever worked on a puzzle for hours and been baffled by a seemingly missing piece? Then someone walked by, picked up that very piece, and said, "Oh, here's a piece for your puzzle."

Life is like that. One person finds a "missing" piece of a spiritual puzzle while someone else finds another. Eventually the puzzle begins to take shape.

I am now finding pieces to the puzzle of life that for much of my seventy-six years had escaped me. If I can show you where a few pieces fit into your puzzle, then you can go on to find even more for yourself. I pray that your adventure will be as exciting as mine. The more pieces I find, the more inspired I am to find even more.

Moving Toward Our Destination

This brings me to a piece that recently fell into place in my puzzle. I say "fell into place" because I didn't find it. Figuratively speaking, the Holy Spirit looked over my shoulder and brought the following questions to my mind: Why did my father see things that no one else in his hospital room could see, and why did my grandmother hear music that I couldn't hear? Why have thousands of people returned from near-death experiences to report similar experiences?

I have come to a much clearer understanding that our physical bodies are merely temporary homes for our eternal spirits. Humankind was corrupted when Adam and Eve sinned, so God drew a curtain between us and what we could see and hear in the spiritual realm. But as our physical bodies approach death, this curtain begins to lift.

Death is seldom instantaneous. The heart flutters, the flow of blood decreases and finally the body dies.

The spirit is then released to embark on its journey into eternity.

This is not a geographical journey, however, for time, space and distance do not exist in eternity. The spirit is released into quite a different realm, a realm that you and I do not see.

The process of aging is a new experience for me, and much of what I am learning is quite new. But it seems that as my natural body moves toward its ultimate destination, my spirit is becoming able to see, hear, and understand new things. As my father lay dying, his spirit was able to see into a different world right there in the hospital room. Years later when my grandmother approached death, she heard music that filled the room with heavenly melodies.

But moving toward physical death is not the only way to see more of the spiritual world. First John 2:15 tells us: *Do not love the world or the things in the world. If anyone loves the world, the love of the Father is not in him*. This verse once seemed somewhat negative to me. It seemed to warn, "Don't do fun things or God will punish you." Now I see it as a positive exhortation to help us find the best things that God has to offer.

The Holy Spirit whispers in my ear: *The things of this world that you see, hear and feel can keep you from seeing into the spiritual world*. It seems that nearly *everything* that the flesh loves can be the means of keeping us from seeing and understanding spiritual things: Money, success, fame, pleasure – the list could go on and on. Jesus tries to help us understand that we can enjoy this life to the absolute maximum if we turn our backs on things cherished by the flesh. He wants to help us, but for much of my life I thought His ways were a burden to bear. I wish that long ago I had understood the truth of His words: *For My yoke is easy and My burden is light* (Matt. 11:30).

Getting older may seem to have many disadvantages, but heed these words of encouragement from Joel 2:28: *It shall come to pass . . . that I will pour out My Spirit on all flesh . . . your old men shall dream dreams*. I believe that my dreams have taught me new things.

In one dream I saw a young man who was deeply in love with a young woman. When he tried to talk with her, she shunned him. But the young man wasn't upset. He tried three more times to talk to her but still she avoided him. Then he said, "I know you don't want to talk with me, but I don't understand why."

"I don't trust you," she said.

"That's all right," he replied, "God has given me a great love for you, and all I want is for you to be happy. Some day He may give you a great love for me. Please know that I would never do anything to hurt you. If you need my help for any reason, please let me know."

The young man was perfectly content for the young woman to go her way; all he wanted was for her to be happy.

When I awoke I prayed for understanding. The Holy Spirit gave me this revelation: God loves us and wants to communicate with us. But if we prefer not to have fellowship with Him, He will not force Himself on us. He knows how much He could help us, but He wants us to *want* His presence. Often we are afraid to trust Him because we think He wants to make our lives difficult.

Reactions to Faith

Have you ever realized how completely our bodies react to what our minds believe? If you were sure that a murderer was pounding on your door trying to get into your home, how would you react?

Your heart would beat faster. Your stomach, skin,

muscles, and every nerve in your body would react. What you believe is of vital importance.

What if the supposed intruder pounding on your door turned out to be a close friend? Your heart, stomach, skin, muscles and nerves would then have no reason to be upset. They had simply reacted to what you believed at the time.

Faith acts in exactly the same way. Your body reacts to *what you believe*.

If you learn to trust God, your faith can defeat your fears. Do not wait until some great danger threatens before you learn to practice trusting God. Instead, why not practice with small, everyday things?

A tiny battery charger I had used only a few days earlier was nowhere to be found. A painstaking search through twelve boxes in our garage produced no results.

The next day I searched even longer – through boxes, behind boxes, under shelves – and anywhere I might have placed the charger. By then I was tempted to be afraid that I wouldn't find it and that I would have to buy a new one. Then I thought, Now is the time to rejoice and believe that God is using this to bless me.

The next day I searched again and kept saying, "Thank You, Lord. You are using this to bless me. There is no reason to be afraid that I've lost the charger. All I need to do is to praise You."

That didn't produce the lost item, so I continued to pray, "Lord, if You want me to find this thing, You could easily tell me where it is. But if not, I will keep on being glad."

Suddenly the thought came to my mind: Look in the trunk of the car.

I had no recollection that the charger had ever been in the trunk of my car, so there was no reason for it to be there. Oh, well, I'd better look anyway, I thought. And there it was!

What if the charger had not been in the car? No matter, because I was in a win-win situation. If I hadn't found the lost item, I would have bought a new one, believing that God was using the entire incident for my good.

Each time we learn to trust Him, the stronger our confidence becomes. Believing that God is in control of small matters prepares us to have faith when we encounter major problems.

Stress is nearly always based on fear. Peace of mind is based on our faith that God is in control of every situation. Jesus said, *Peace I leave with you, My peace I give to you; not as the world gives do I give to you. Let not your heart be troubled, neither let it be afraid* (John 14:27).

Having peace of mind over a lost battery charger may seem trivial, but what if we learn to have faith in every situation of our lives? That is worth learning, and is a way of life that I strongly recommend. God doesn't want us to be afraid of anything, big or small, and He will help us if we will make the effort to learn how to trust Him.

I have come to believe that what I have is exactly what I need, so if I need to lose something, I will! And if I need the spiritual exercise of dealing with an irritable person, God will send that person to me. My purpose in life is not to judge that person or to be upset. It is to believe that God is using that person to bless me.

What a great relief this discovery was to give me! It's helped me so much that I pray that you, too, will understand this principle and put it to work for you. Then an irritable spouse, child, co-worker, rude driver or shopper, will work *for you*. Even your ill-tempered and demanding boss can be made to work for you.

On the other hand, if we choose to be irritable or afraid, or to feel harassed by our fellow human beings, God will allow us to hasten our physical bodies on to their untimely demise. Fear is so powerful that once we take it into our hearts, it can quickly undermine, then destroy our health and happiness.

Life can seem eternal until we experience the first symptoms of aging. A little ache here, a pain there, and we begin to confront our mortality.

Then the thought comes, *Will I ever suffer like those elderly people?* We may try to ignore this distressing thought, but it won't go away. Eventually this fear works its way into our consciousness: What will happen to me? Will I become disabled? Will I spend my final years in a hospital with people who are old and dying? Such fearful thoughts can be destructive to our peace of mind even while we are still young.

Fear says, "If you do this or that, you might lose your health. If you rise early to pray, or try to fast or serve the Lord too strenuously, you might shorten your life."

Jesus advised us to live life as if we had already lost it. It's gone. We no longer have it. But in losing life, we gain it. Our health then belongs to God, and *because we have given it to Him*, Satan can't take it away. Our faith is the ultimate weapon that defeats all of Satan's devices.

Jesus told God, *I have finished the work which You have given Me to do* (John 17:4). Having fulfilled His earthly mission, why should He stay longer? Why should you and I live any longer than is necessary for us to finish our tasks? If we serve God, He alone determines when it is time for us to depart this earth. When He designed your DNA, He gave you the exact physical makeup that you need to complete your mission!

Unite with me, then, in learning how to have the kind of faith that defeats fear. Believe me, we will need it. Whatever one's age, now is the time to learn how to be victorious over fear.

FROM FEAR TO FAITH

Chapter 15

When God Says "Don't Do It"
He Means "Don't Do It"

Unseen germs are the cause of many diseases. These enemies of health went undetected for hundreds of years; even the most educated physicians had no knowledge of them. After operating on patients, these doctors wiped their scalpels on soiled towels. The infections that resulted killed countless people.

Louis Pasteur (1822-95), French chemist and microbiologist, proved that microorganisms cause disease, and that each microbe derives from a previous one; i.e., one feeds upon the other. These invisible microbes have killed millions upon millions of people

"Spiritual germs" are also unseen, yet they can infect and defeat every one of us if we do not protect ourselves. These germs are also passed from one person to another.

God promised Abraham that he would be the father of a great nation that would one day live in the Promised Land. But after hundreds of years, that promise had still not been fulfilled.

The Israelites were slaves in Egypt for four hundred years. During that time, many generations might have sat around evening fires and wondered if God's promise would ever be a reality.

Nearly five hundred years after Abraham received God's promise, Moses arrived in Egypt to lead his people out of slavery. They were finally on their way to the Promised Land!

As always, however, God's promise of deliverance was conditional. He required that His people trust Him. They didn't, of course, preferring instead to complain about God's treatment of them.

Paul looked back on their failure to trust God and gave a stern admonition:

Don't murmur against God and his dealings with you, as some of them did, for that is why God sent his Angel to destroy them. All these things happened to them as examples - as object lessons to us - to warn us against doing the same things; they were written down so that we could read about them and learn from them . . . So be careful. If you are thinking, Oh, I would never behave like that - let this be a warning to you. For you too may fall into sin (1 Cor. 10:10-12 TLB).

I am afraid that many of us have ignored God's object lesson. We can "behave like that" if we don't know what the Israelites did that caused them so much trouble. We can be involved in their sin of complaining. This sin can lie undetected as it works its destruction of our faith. At times it can cause us to feel powerless and defeated, and we wonder why we feel so discouraged. That's why Paul warns us about what happened to the Israelites, so we don't behave like they did.

God wanted Abraham's children to live in peace in their Promised Land. Instead, they lived and died in the desert because they refused to trust Him. God wants Christians today to dwell their own "Promised Land," but if we complain and rebel, we will languish in a dry and barren spiritual desert of our own making.

Paul recognized that Christians of his day were making dreadful mistakes. Like the Israelites, they were complaining and rebelling against God. Alarmed, Paul warned Christians not to respond with, "Oh, I would never behave like that."

Only a few days after the Israelites marched triumphantly out of Egypt carrying the spoils of God's mighty deliverance, they faltered. They did something that we should avoid doing at all costs. But we won't avoid this error unless we understand the nature of this hidden spiritual germ.

The people were thirsty but there was no water to drink. Who was in charge of providing it? Well, who had led them out into the desert? Moses! It was his fault!

The people growled and complained to Moses. 'Give us water!' they wailed. 'Quiet!' Moses commanded. 'Are you trying to test God's patience with you?' (Ex. 17:2 TLB).

They might have thought, What does God have to do with it? Moses is the one who led us out here to die.

Moses insisted that they were speaking not against him but against God. That's curious, isn't it? They complained to a man, but in God's eyes they were speaking against Him.

But, tormented by thirst, they cried out, 'Why did you ever take us out of Egypt? Why did you bring us here to die, with our children?' (Ex. 17:3 TLB*).*

Angry and afraid, they cried, "Don't you even care about our little children?" It's easy to clothe our complaints by claiming that our concerns are for our children, or for the elderly, poor, or sick. Actually, however, our complaints are usually centered on a selfish, "See what's happening to me, my family and my friends."

The people of Israel argued against God and tempted him to slay them by saying, 'Is Jehovah going to take care of us or not?' (Ex. 17:7 TLB).

Why did God prevent the thirsty people from finding water? Certainly He knew that after three days they would soon begin to die. God did know the problem, but for some reason He chose to temporarily deny water to about three million people. What was that reason? Perhaps His objective was quite simple.

Among the millions assembled may have been some who still believed in the Egyptian gods. They might have needed to be eliminated. When the people continued to complain, God reminded them of what they had asked Moses in Exodus 17:3: *Why is it you have brought us up out of Egypt, to kill us and our children and our livestock with thirst?* Finally in Numbers 14:28-29, God said, *Just as you have spoken in My hearing, so I will do to you: The carcasses of you who have complained against Me shall fall in this wilderness, all of you who were numbered, . . . from twenty years old and above.* This rebuke by God reveals that He is not pleased when His children complain about the trials He asks them to endure.

All the adults except for Caleb and Joshua, died in the desert. They would never enter the Promised Land. Five hundred years of waiting and hoping had been wiped out. We may think such a punishment unreasonable – disproportionate to the offense. Should our failure to trust God be punished by a life sentence without parole?

The sentence of death for eating a piece of fruit in the Garden of Eden may also seem unfair. Our sinful minds usually refuse to accept that disobedience to God should be so severely punished. We can always find some "reasonable" excuse for our actions. But we are cautioned in 1 Corinthians 10:10 (TLB): *Don't murmur against God and his dealings with you, as some of them did, for that is why God sent his Angel to destroy them.*

For His own reasons, God allowed the Israelites to be without water for three days. Going three days without liquids can cause severe hardships. The people suffered greatly and needed help, but more than anything else they needed to learn to trust God. Perhaps that is why He withheld the water they needed. Eventually He gave them plenty of water, but by then the people had already proven that they wouldn't trust Him to do what He thought was best for them.

They complained, too, when their diet consisted only of manna. Seven days a week, nothing but manna. Think a moment about your reactions to the trials in your life. Were your reactions like those of Moses' flock?

'Oh, that we were back in Egypt,' they moaned, 'and that the Lord had killed us there! For there we had plenty to eat. But now you have brought us into this wilderness to kill us with starvation' (Ex. 16:3 TLB).

How often have you grumbled about the things you had to eat and drink? You probably didn't grumble against God. You probably grumbled against people, or your situation, without realizing that God permitted you to be in that predicament.

Faith is the exact opposite of complaining. Faith says, "God is in charge of everything, and He is working out everything for my good." If we believe that God is using our problems for our good, we show the quality of faith for which He looks.

When unpleasant things happen, we would do well to meditate on Ephesians 5:20 (TLB): *Always give thanks for everything*. We don't like to believe that such a command is necessary; we prefer instead to make our own judgments of what is permissible in our case.

Abraham is repeatedly honored in the Bible for his unusual faith: *Abraham believed God even though such a promise just couldn't come to pass!* (Rom. 4:18 TLB). The King James Version says that he *against hope he believed in hope.*

If we have no money, if friends and family have deserted us, if we or a loved one is in pain, it might seem that God isn't working in our situation for our good. For years, Abraham saw no evidence that God would fulfill His promise. But Abraham refused to doubt: *Abraham never doubted. He believed God, for his faith and trust grew ever stronger, and he praised God* (Rom. 4:20 TLB).

Not only did Abraham refuse to doubt; he was fully persuaded: *He was completely sure that God was well able to do anything he promised* (Rom. 4:21 TLB).

As Romans 5:3-5 (TLB) tells us:

We can rejoice, too, when we run into problems and trials for we know that they are good for us - they help us learn to be patient. And patience develops strength of character in us and helps us trust God more each time we use it until finally our hope and faith are strong and steady. Then, when that happens, we are able to hold our heads high no matter what happens and know that all is well.

The Israelites believed that their problems and trials would not work for their good, so they looked for someone to criticize. As a result, they lost their chance of a lifetime to learn to trust God no matter what should happen. They died in the desert instead of enjoying the abundant fruits of the Promised Land.

Jesus said, *Don't criticize* (Matt. 7:1 TLB). But when we see the flaws in other people, we often prefer to be disobedient and we think, Let me help you get that speck out of your eye.

Jesus had a one-word reaction to anyone who was critical of others: *Hypocrite!* (Matt. 7:5 TLB). We have a hundred opportunities every day to criticize others. After all, we reason, they need it.

During my seventy-six years on the earth, I have criticized many people. I have even criticized the same person many times. As I look back I realize that about 99 percent of the time my criticism did not help those people.

I, too, have been criticized often, and I can't recall even one time when it made me feel good, and too often it didn't help me to become a better person.

Don't be upset when people criticize you, because even Jesus was criticized. Others found fault with Him when:

- He ate with people of ill repute (Mark 2:16).
- His disciples didn't fast (Matt. 9:14).
- He worked on the Sabbath (Matt. 12:10-11).
- He let people crowd around Him when He hadn't taken time to eat (Mark 3:20–21).
- He went to sleep when the disciples needed Him to keep the boat afloat (Matt. 8:24).
- He said a dead person was only sleeping (Luke 8:52).
- He let His disciples eat without washing their hands (Mark 7:5).
- He permitted unholy people to touch Him (Luke 7:39).
- He let people waste money on Him (John 12:5,7).
- He called God His Father (Matt. 26:65–66).

Romans 14:13 (TLB) urges, *Don't criticize each other any more.* Some Christians may believe that God has given them a "special anointing" to find fault with others. Somewhat like "Card-Carrying Criticizers." But James 4:12 (TLB) asks, *What right do you have to judge or criticize others?*.

How about your spouse? Even if he or she is nearly perfect, you could still find many opportunities every day to criticize. But if you give in to that urge, you will move farther into a spiritual desert.

James 5:9 (TLB) declares, *Don't grumble about each other*. We will remain powerless until we learn how to stop being critical of others. There will always be people living and working with or around us, who need to improve. Always! Why are they there? Because we need to learn how to resist the temptation to criticize!

Such people supply us with exactly what we need. The Israelites didn't believe that, so they criticized Moses. But they didn't get away with it, and neither will we.

Criticism is like germs. It takes everything that is bad in us and makes it even worse. Every time we find fault with people or God, we move ourselves farther into the desert. And like the Israelites, we will stay there until we learn – or die.

Yes, the Israelites were still God's children even after they disobeyed Him. For forty years He miraculously supplied their food, water, and clothing. Their refusal to believe, however, prevented them from entering into the life that God had planned for them. Even if you and I complain and refuse to believe that God is working in our lives, we will remain children of God. But many of His promised blessings will be denied us until we learn to obey Him. Like it or not, that's the way it is.

Praising God for everything that happens to us causes us to enter into a deep, satisfying, restful trust in God. It causes us to believe that God will use all of life's bitter and painful experiences for our good to produce His will in us. And that is the foundation for living in incredible joy.

A chemist can take a poisonous ingredient and modify it until it becomes a healing medicine. God wants us to take the evil things that attack us, such as the temptation to criticize others, and compel them to help us. Why would anyone refuse such an incredible offer?

Job 5:17 states, *Happy is the man whom God corrects; therefore do not despise the chastening of the Almighty*. Each of us needs to learn how to be that happy man or woman, and we can, once we learn to believe that God always keeps His promises. As our faith rests on His joy, our joy becomes incredible!

Chapter 16

Power Works

Joshua – what a man!

To understand power and how it works, consider Joshua. While others were complaining, he was learning. Living in the wilderness on a one-item diet caused millions of people to complain. But Joshua did the unusual; he didn't grumble. And God selected Joshua to lead His people.

Joshua demonstrated the incredible power that you and I can have if we help our faith to grow. Joshua spoke to the Lord in the presence of the Israelites:

Sun, stand still . . .
So the sun stood still,
And the moon stopped,
Till the people had revenge
Upon their enemies . . .
The sun stood still in the midst of heaven, and did not hasten to go down for about a whole day (Josh. 10:12–13).

Think of it! What had to happen to cause the sun to stand still? The universe is designed to move, and is held together by the laws of gravity. Billions of stars swirl through space, and each depends on the gravitational pull of all the others. When the sun stood still, something awesome had to happen.

Joshua probably knew nothing about gravity and the other forces of the universe, or about the motion of the Earth. He didn't need to. He had learned to believe that God would take care of whatever needed to be done.

Although Joshua did not realize the awesome power needed to stop the sun and moon, that didn't affect God's willingness to act. This event reveals God's willingness to move heaven and Earth to solve any problem we may have.

So what if every known law has to be changed?

So what if our problems seem great?

So what if our faith seems weak?

If you and I believe that God will make any problem work for our good, He will use His awesome power to reward our trust in Him.

If He has to change people and situations or alter present and future events, is that any different from what He did for Joshua? So what if He has to take an evil scheme devised by Satan and make it work for our good?

I began to examine some of my own prayers, and discovered that sometimes the prayers themselves revealed that I didn't believe God would answer them.

Here is an illustration. I prayed, "God, please help me to feel better," with a plaintive whine in my voice. There was nothing wrong with my words, but my tone of voice revealed that I didn't really expect God to help me. So my prayer left me feeling discouraged and depressed.

Then I practiced praying until the tone in my words reflected the joy and conviction that God *would* help me. My prayers did not sound "doubting and double-minded." Please experiment with a prayer of your own, and see if you can make it sound as if you really expect God to answer. I believe you will be pleased as you see prayer and faith taking on a new and happy meaning. As your attitude changes from one of fear to one of believing, you will eventually experience new delight.

If our faith is too weak to ask for a major miracle, we should ask for things we believe God *will do*. Instead of saying, "God, please give me perfect health," we may need to say, "I ask You to bring healing to me. Yes, God, I really do believe You are healing me." That's a mustard seed–sized faith that can grow day by day.

Jesus said, *Whatever things you ask in prayer, believing, you will receive* (Matt. 21:22). Notice He said, *Ask in prayer, believing*. He emphasized the importance of believing while we are asking.

In Mark 11:24, He said, *Therefore I say to you, whatever things you ask when you pray, believe that you receive them*. I have seen this principle at work when people have asked me to pray for them. If their problems were severe, my heart often strained as I anxiously hoped that God would hear and answer. It's extremely difficult not to be anxious when a huge problem stares you in the face.

Sometimes I have prayed for people without knowing anything about their problems. These prayers held no doubt or uncertainty, and at the same time I sensed that the Holy Spirit was quickening my heart with confidence. I really believed that God was answering their prayers. Miracles occurred at those times when there was no doubting.

Remember all the Bible characters who grew in faith? They didn't see immediate answers to big prayers, but they kept asking, in faith believing.

Luke 2:52 says that, *Jesus increased in wisdom and stature, and in favor with God and men*. Think of that. Even Jesus had to increase in favor with God. He increased in favor with God by His daily obedience. We, too, can increase in favor and, if we are willing and obedient, we, too, can learn how to honor God's promises.

Incredible power belongs to those who are willing and eager to do whatever is necessary to grow in faith. God's gift of faith is alive in us, and is a gift we can use to defeat any doubts or fears that may lurk within us.

The absolute certainty that your Creator hears and is answering your prayers will be one of the most satisfying, exciting, and enjoyable experiences you will ever have. Jesus assured us that, *I give you the authority . . . over all the power of the enemy* (Luke 10:19). That's incredible!

Chapter 17

Have No Fear, Joy Is Here

Faith and trust in God grow in each person's heart in different ways, just as the same seeds grow differently in various soils. Some folks focus their attention on Bible verses that promise healing, and they receive healing. Others fix their attention on believing that God will provide them exactly what He knows is best for them, and they too receive healing.

God isn't concerned with *how* we grow in faith; He is concerned that we do it. No procedure devised by humans is perfect, because human beings are fallible creatures. Whatever approach we use, God is pleased when we come to the place where our trust in Him increases. It is my objective here to do whatever I can to help you enjoy a life of faith in Christ, a life of faith that will enable you to move from fear toward faith.

Some people face problems that you and I may never encounter, but our goal is the same: to learn to have the kind of faith that works, whatever the situation.

What happens when a man becomes so fearful of what may happen tomorrow that he cannot cope with the present? He may contemplate suicide. Unless he finds a solution to his problems, he may eventually end his life.

Lloyd's of London, the giant insurance conglomerate, is in the business of insuring multi-billion dollar projects. The many worldwide natural disasters that occurred during the 1990's caused the firm to lose a reported twelve billion dollars.

Executives in British corporations are often individually liable for corporate losses. Many directors of Lloyd's of London are said to have lost everything they owned, including their homes. All of the men had been fabulously wealthy. Losing everything they had caused a reported thirty-two executives to be so afraid of the future that they took their own lives.

One of the directors read my book *Prison to Praise*. He was so impressed that he had his secretary contact me to see if I could come to London to speak to the other directors.

On the appointed day I stood in a magnificent mahogany-paneled study facing an audience of impeccably dressed businessmen. Although they appeared to be eminently successful, their faces betrayed their abject misery. And they were miserable! Maybe they resented being required to waste their time listening to some American author when they could have been tending to important business matters. For whatever reason, it was obvious that they were most unhappy.

I spoke with all the enthusiasm and joy that I could muster. I used illustrations that would usually bring smiles to an audience. Nothing worked. My audience grew increasingly restive. My joy, I noticed, seemed to be making them even more resentful.

Lord, what can I do? Please help me. I'm wasting my time and theirs.

Then I heard an inner whisper, Teach them the song that I taught you.

I thought, *Oh, Lord, I must be misunderstanding You. Surely You don't want me to teach them that song. They won't understand! They will think I'm really stupid!*

But I received no further guidance. All I could do was to stop my planned message, and ask "How many of you know the song 'London Bridge Is Falling Down'?"

There was an uneasy silence as the men glanced at one another. They were obviously baffled. What is this idiot doing now? No one made any effort to answer my question.

The only thing I knew to do then was to sing the little song the Lord had taught me. It was to the tune of 'London Bridge Is Falling Down':

God is working for my good,
for my good, for my good.
God is working for my good;
yes, He really is.

As I sang, I saw a slight smile on one man's face – ever so slight.

Then I urged, "Please sing with me." And off I went again: God is working for my good . . .

No one sang, but more men were smiling and the tension was leaving their faces. I sang again. By the time I was through nearly everyone was smiling. Something had definitely happened. The men were hearing me!

God often uses childlike things to accomplish His purposes. Remember David's encounter with Goliath? David had only a slingshot, but he won the battle. David said to the Philistine, *You come to me with a sword, with a spear, and with a javelin. But I come to you in the name of the Lord of hosts . . . The Lord will deliver you into my hand . . . that all the earth may know that there is a God in Israel* (1 Sam. 17:45–46).

By the time I switched back to my message I had a changed audience. They listened attentively to me. When I was finished, three of the directors requested copies of *Prison to Praise* to send to branch offices throughout the world.

Please hear me, dear reader. That little song is true. It's true for me, and God wants it to be true for you, too. He wants us to trust Him. He gave us the instrument of faith that we can use to claim victory over every kind of fear.

Since that day in London, I've been teaching that same song to thousands of people. Many of them report remarkable changes in their lives as they sing it and believe it. Physicians and psychologists have been teaching it to their patients. One psychologist told me that for months she had been trying to help an especially depressed patient. After this doctor read about this song in *Praise News*, a free newsletter that Mary and I send out every month, she taught it to the patient and prescribed that the patient sing it several times every day.

The following week the patient returned to the doctor with her husband. He wanted to thank her doctor for the remarkable change that had taken place in his wife. As of this writing, that healthy change has continued.

Make that little song a way of life for yourself. God will use it to melt fear from your heart and strengthen your faith in His promises. It may seem silly, but if it works, why knock it? Sometimes I change the words to:

God, You're working for my good,
  for my good, for my good.
God, You're working for my good;
  yes, You really are.

If at first I don't feel faith stirring in my heart, I sing it again and again until I do. Sooner or later my heart begins to sing, and my heart goes from fear to faith.

It is difficult to be upset about anything if we really believe that God is working for our good. That is why Joseph could so freely say to his brothers: *You meant evil against me; but God meant it for good* (Gen. 50:20).

Chapter 18

The Smallest Seed

How strong is your desire to have faith that has power? Stories about other people's miraculous faith are encouraging, but it is far better to learn how faith works and how God designed it to do so.

For years I repeated certain prayers that accomplished nothing. I told God, other people, and myself that I believed a certain prayer had been answered. But in my heart I did not really believe that my problem had been resolved. In my fifty years as a minister I have talked with and read letters from thousands who have had the same problem.

The solution is simple: we must learn to believe! That is, we must learn to believe in our hearts so we are no longer trying to fool our innermost thoughts. Let's be sure of one thing: We can never fool God; He always knows exactly what we truly believe:

You may be surprised to learn that we cannot lie to ourselves. When we earnestly and sincerely try to believe, what we really don't believe, we must remember that our bodies have complicated, sensitive and intricately woven components, each seeming to "know" much about the others.

Consider the lie detector test. If you were tested and lied in response to a simple question such as, "Have you ever broken the speed limit?" it would register whether or not you told the truth. If you answered no, your body would react, "You just told a lie." Think of what your inner response would be if you were asked a very emotional question!

Our conscious minds may not know exactly what is going on, but *something* inside us does. Our bodies function somewhat like a computer. If we entered 10,000 or even 1,000,000 correct keystrokes and one incorrect one for a complex mathematical formula on how to send a rocket to Mars, the computer would not give us the response we seek. We could get angry, and want to demolish the machine, but it would not respond properly until we corrected that one keystroke.

We can tell ourselves, others, and God, that we believe in, trust in, and rely on Him, but if indeed we do *not*, something within us says, *You aren't telling the truth!* Proverbs 20:27 tells us that *the spirit of a man is the lamp of the Lord.* God sees what we truly believe in our innermost hearts. If we understand this, then we won't be nearly so confused about some of our unanswered prayers.

I do not mean that God is saying, "I won't listen to you because you aren't doing it right." He knows our frailties. But we can't fool the innermost part of ourselves that knows exactly what we really think and feel.

In Matthew 9:29, Jesus said, *According to your faith let it be to you.* The opposite is equally true. Jesus could just as well have said, "According to your fear let it be to you." He was saying that as we believe, so it is done. Therefore, it is imperative that we learn exactly how to believe and how to be delivered from fear.

My participation in World War II (as an infantry soldier in the Eighty-second Airborne Division), the Korean Conflict, and the Dominican Republic gave me many intense experiences in what it is like to be afraid.

In 1966 the Army once again transported me from my relatively comfortable and safe environment in the U.S. to the Vietnam Conflict. During my 365 days in that agonizing war, I frequently visited men who had been severely injured when a truck or jeep ran over a land mine. When I went to see them, I rode in a jeep through some of those same deadly areas. I became intensely aware that I, too, might not leave Vietnam in one piece, and I had abundant reason to go from fear to even greater fear. If my faith had not grown, I would have become as fearful as some of the other officers. They simply avoided all possible danger, contriving every conceivable excuse to stay as far as possible from harm's way.

As an Army private in World War II, I went where I was told to go; as a lieutenant colonel chaplain, however, I went where I *believed* I should go. That required the strengthening of my faith. Would God protect me even when I wasn't being forced to take such risks? I believed that He would.

We need to examine many aspects of the fears we have stored within us. This may require us to change one or more things about the people we are. Then our faith is released in a new way. When we say, "I believe!" our "inner computer" runs a verification check. If everything comes out correctly, each part of the body and spirit cooperates to release God's joy, peace, and healing.

When a Christian says, "I have all the faith in the world, but God isn't answering my prayers," he is making contradictory statements. When someone says, "God is not answering my prayers," he is also saying, "I do not believe God is answering." When he says that God isn't answering his prayers, he is saying, in essence, that God is doing exactly what he himself believes!

Sometimes our faith is crippled by our failure to pray within the boundaries of God's will. For example, it would be sheer folly to ask God to give us another person's spouse.

Once we realize how crucial it is to truly believe what we say, we will concentrate on learning *how* to believe. This we can, and must, learn!

The Power of a Seed

God created each of us with many abilities, one of which is the capacity to believe. Jesus told us to have faith as a mustard seed, which in His time was thought to be the smallest seed. He said to the disciples, *I say to you, if you have faith as a mustard seed, you will say to this mountain, 'Move from here to there,' and it will move; and nothing will be impossible for you* (Matt. 17:20).

This analogy is simple, yet so profound that it has often been misunderstood. Many Christians feel that Jesus was saying that even the smallest amount of faith could remove a mountain. But He couldn't have meant that! Since He spoke those words, not one Christian, to the best of my knowledge, has ever had sufficient faith to remove a mountain by believing that it would move. Rather, He was telling us that the nature of faith is like that of a seed; when cared for properly, it can grow. A grain of sand is perhaps larger than a mustard seed, but the sand will never increase in size.

Jesus never spoke sternly toward people who had only a small amount of faith unless they had ample opportunities to grow in faith yet refused to make the effort.

He did, however, speak harshly to the scribes and Pharisees who gloried in their own righteousness and knowledge of the Scripture, but did not believe in Him as the promised Messiah. When the elders, chief priests and scribes asked Him if He was the Christ, He said, *If I tell you, you will by no means believe* (Luke 22:67).

Jesus also spoke critically to a man who was classified as a "nobleman." Jesus said to him, *Unless you people see signs and wonders, you will by no means believe* (John 4:48). Jesus honored the man's request, but made it clear that faith *without* physical evidence should be our goal.

Jesus thought that His disciple Thomas should have learned to have faith in Him, but Thomas would not believe that Jesus had been resurrected from the dead. Jesus said to him, *Blessed are those who have not seen and yet have believed* (John 20:29).

When Jesus addressed His disciples, He spoke to men who had lived with Him, broken bread with Him, heard Him teach and witnesses His many miracles, yet who still lacked the faith He thought they should have had. In Matthew 17:17, Jesus was referring to His disciples when He said, *O faithless and perverse generation, how long shall I be with you? How long shall I bear with you?* These were indeed harsh words, but He thought these favored men should have learned something after the many opportunities He had given them.

To Philip Jesus said, *Have I been with you so long, and yet you have not known Me, Philip? He who has seen Me has seen the Father; so how can you say, 'Show us the Father'?* (John 14:9).

Peter had actually walked on water, but he became afraid and sank. To him Jesus said, *O you of little faith, why did you doubt?* (Matt. 14:31).

If we have been Christians for years yet still rest comfortably in our lack of faith, we need to reassess our progress and seek new ways to go from fear to faith.

All of us are all subject to fears of one kind or another, but we can learn how to be delivered from them if only we will develop our faith. My own faith is far weaker than I would like it to be, but I am determined to do whatever I can to strengthen it. I've learned that if I patiently endure every painful circumstance and believe that God is always working for my good (Rom. 8:28), my faith steadily increases.

If you are living in a painful situation, you can now begin to believe that God is working for your good. You can claim this promise for your past, present, and all future situations. Romans 12:12 (TLB) gives us a marvelous way to deal with the future: *Be glad for all God is planning for you.*

Jesus likened faith to the tiny mustard seed that grows until it produces a bush that can reach as high as eight feet. Often its branches are large enough to use as wood. Like the mustard seed, our faith can and will grow if we will nurture it. When it matures, nothing is impossible.

It takes six to eight *years* for a mustard seed to grow into an eight-foot bush. If it does not reach its full height in a day, a month, or a year, would the wise farmer dig it up and throw it away as useless? No! Faith is supposed to grow in the same way – gradually.

If we reject our faith because we feel that it is not great enough, we will never know the awesome power of faith that changes us and the world around us.

Faith that bears fruit must be nurtured hour by hour, day by day. How is faith nurtured? By *choosing* to believe that it is there and growing, even when you don't feel it. "But," you may ask, "How do I know that I have a seed of faith to begin with?" Paul answers this question in Romans 12:3: *God has dealt to each one a measure of faith.*

Faith is a gift from God not something we deserve or are entitled to. Some Christians labor under the delusion that either we believe or we don't believe. In reality, we believe in varying degrees.

Growth is in the very nature of a seed. A seed can't make itself grow; it needs sun and rain. But that is not all it needs. The patient farmer must also cultivate the soil. He knows well the truth of James 2:20: *Faith without works is dead*.

God gives you and me faith, but it will not grow unless we learn how to cultivate it. Without cultivation it will remain a tiny seed for our entire lives.

Steps to Faith

Somehow we all must find a way to begin each day with a spiritual exercise that will cause our faith to grow. For example, we could read or quote Scriptures (there are many in this book) that emphasize the victory that is ours in Christ.

Whatever we elect to do, we need to do it nearly 365 days a year. Otherwise we soon discover that we seldom, or never, do it. Consistency is necessary.

I've been told that the body requires twenty minutes of vigorous exercise for it to circulate and cleanse all of its blood. Spiritual exercise also requires time.

Years ago I began going for a walk the first thing every morning. As I walk up the steep hill near our home, I concentrate on hearing whatever the Holy Spirit wants to tell me. For about a year, those early morning walks required much discipline. I could always think of a good reason why I should skip my spiritual exercise for that day. Now, I feel disappointed if something prevents me from enjoying that special time with God. I urgently desire to learn how I can best be used to build His kingdom.

Jesus knew by age twelve that it was important for Him to be engaged in His Father's business. His teachings urge us to follow His example.

Jesus selected a mountain as the object to be moved by faith. Why? Because of its immense size. By selecting a mountain, Jesus was saying, "By your faith you can defeat the biggest problems that can ever come into your life."

A dry seed cannot crack a solid rock. But as that seed grows, it can eventually split the rock.

A huge rock beside our home was about twenty-five feet long and twenty feet wide. Long ago a pine tree seed had fallen into a tiny crevice and grown to about fifty feet high. In the process it split that great rock.

In the same way, faith, while still the size of a mustard seed, will not solve a mountain-sized problem. Yet as it grows, it will. This gives us all hope.

No matter how difficult our problems may be, we can find the solution if we have faith.

If you were to encounter an enormous "mountain" such as a life-threatening cancer, a mustard seed–sized faith could not instantly remove it. You may have observed people striving to believe that God had healed a cancer. But if their faith was still the size of a mustard seed, they remained ill and became discouraged.

That is why we need situations that nurture our faith. If God in His love gives us these opportunities to mature in our faith, we can learn, persistently and patiently, to declare that in each and every situation He is working all things for our good.

Lessons in the Sky

When I was thirteen years old, I knew that someday I wanted to fly an airplane. For years afterward I lost no opportunity to study airplanes while they were on the ground. When I saw one in flight high above the earth I never failed to gaze longingly at it. That flying airplanes might be dangerous never entered my mind, but a couple of harrowing incidents in the military educated me quickly.

During World War II, I was a passenger on a military aircraft that was over the ocean and on fire. Would the gas tanks explode? Would we crash into the icy water and perish? We were terrified, and even now I remember that some of the men were unashamedly praying.

The pilot shut off one of the two engines and put the plane into a steep dive in an effort to extinguish the fire. He succeeded, and we sputtered onward to eventually land on one engine. How frightened was I? Exceedingly!

After exiting the plane we sat along a small, isolated dirt runway until trucks arrived to take us to our destination. The pilot never bothered to tell us privates what had happened. Perhaps he needed authorization because of our mission.

Years later, as an Army chaplain, I visited a pilot who had crashed into the flagpole at the post headquarters. He looked horrible as he lay in his hospital bed. He was in a coma and was being kept alive by several machines. As I stood beside his corpselike body, the thought came to me, *Do I really want to fly airplanes?* If I had given in to those fears, I would have missed the many years that I enjoyed flying. Now I rejoice that God gave me opportunities to be afraid and opportunities to grow in faith that He would protect me.

You may ask, "But what about Christian pilots who have crashed and died? Why didn't God protect them?" It is my conviction that if they were being reasonably cautious, they were scheduled to be with the Lord on that day. They could have met their deaths at any time – while driving an automobile, while exercising – even from a heart attack while asleep Ultimately, when or how we die is not as important as our learning to go from fear to faith.

Each day your faith can grow a little stronger. You may not see it growing, just as you cannot measure a mustard seed's growth after only one day. However, daily growth *does* produce results. You may never face a mountain-sized problem, but it is very likely that someone you know will need extra help. As you exercise the faith you do have, it will grow and grow. Then you will be ready to provide that extra help. God's Word tells us that our faith will overcome the world. No mountain-sized problem is large enough to overwhelm or defeat us: *This is the victory that has overcome the world – our faith* (1 John 5:4).

When faith does not produce instant, visible results, too many Christians become discouraged and quit. To them, faith means, "Pray, and receive an immediate answer."

With no apparent miracle, some folks feel that God is not answering their prayers. Fear then overcomes their faith. If a little mustard plant is plucked from the earth and not replanted, it dies. No amount of sunshine and water can revive it. That's the way God designed it. Likewise, He can and will permit things to happen in our lives that have the *potential* to cause our faith to die. Why does He allow these things to happen? Because He knows that if we choose to respond in faith, our tiny faith will grow larger and stronger. Our part is to nurture the mustard seed-sized faith He gave us – day by day, year by year – for as long as He permits. Our quiet determination is a joy to God. He may allow people or circumstances to knock us down, but only to help us learn that faith can work and grow in us.

Speaking of being knocked down, I once had the experience of being *forced* down. While flying a small airplane with no radio, I became totally lost. I scanned the ground in all directions, seeking reference points that would correspond to those on my map. My search was unavailing, however; I could locate no reference points. The sun had set and darkness was falling. It was my first long-distance flight and I was over completely new territory. I didn't know what to do. In training, my instructor had taught me, "If you become lost, look for a safe place to land." But I was flying over a city; there seemed to be no safe place to land.

After circling round and round, trying to get my bearings, I decided to fly in the general direction of my destination and hope for the best. Darkness seemed to be descending more rapidly than it had come in my entire life! Was I afraid? No doubt about it; I was terrified. How God must have smiled as He saw that I was being prepared to better understand the nature of fear. Maybe He thought, If Merlin is going to write a book about fear someday, he really needs to understand what it's like.

Here at the safety of my desk it's easy for me to ask myself, *Why was I afraid?* Wasn't God taking care of me? At the time, however, it wasn't at all clear to me how intimately God is involved in our lives.

Suddenly something happened that made me even more afraid. Two military aircraft were buzzing around me. Their aggressive maneuvers made it mandatory for me to go in the direction they were herding me. They forced me to what I soon realized was a landing strip. Seeing the safe landing place was a comfort, but I knew something bad was happening. Never before had I been forced to land a plane, especially by military aircraft, and I had never heard of anyone else having had such an experience.

When my plane came to a complete stop I saw military police vehicles racing toward me, their lights flashing. Since I, too, was in the Army, I knew something was wrong. It was. I had been flying over Fort Knox! The people who guard the vast reserves of gold there didn't like unidentified planes flying over them!

What a stern lecture I received! They told me that I had been flying over restricted air space and that they could have shot me down. I expected them to slap handcuffs on me and march me away. But after they had examined my plane, saw I had no radio, and examined my flying logbook, they realized that I was merely a confused lost pilot. The next morning they made sure I knew how to find my way home, and sent me on my way. God had provided me with a problem, let me perspire a little, and then supplied His solution.

I'm convinced that such experiences as this were designed by God to show me how little faith I had and how much I needed to trust that He involves Himself in everything that happens to me. This doesn't mean that He always causes bad things to happen to us just so He can teach us something. I mean that He causes us to be where we need to be so that we can learn whatever it is we need to learn.

Once, during WW II, I was on a troopship in the middle of the Atlantic Ocean. It was night and we were under attack by a German U-boat. All of my "fun" experiences seem to have happened at night. The anxious captain had assembled us on deck so we could gain quicker access to the lifeboats. Even now I can picture the black, foreboding sea, and I remember how frightened we all were. We had heard about the many US ships that had been sunk in the Atlantic and the hundreds of lives that had been lost. The thought of the ship's going down and our being cast into the sea really got my attention, and that, I believe, was all God had in mind for the time being.

We know that God could solve all our problems and change everything with a sweep of His hand, but that isn't His plan. He wants us to believe, continue to believe, then believe some more. What would happen if someone stepped on a little mustard plant? It would strive a little harder to reach back toward the sky. And that is the way our faith grows. Paul spoke proudly of the believers in Thessalonica regarding their *patience and faith in all your persecutions and tribulations* (2 Thes. 1:4).

Practice Believing

Jesus knew that as we practice believing we will nurture our faith, which in turn will produce joy and spiritual strength. To His followers who would not believe, He said, *You are such foolish people! You find it so hard to believe* (Luke 24:25 TLB). Jesus was saddened that mankind would reject the seed of faith and the capacity to grow in believing that He had planted within us.

I do not know how faith works its mysterious ways, but there are, I believe, some things we can observe about it.

Paul wrote to Timothy, *Stir up the gift of God which is in you* (2 Tim.1:6). Our task, then, is to *stir up* our faith into action!

Second, as we use the faith that we have, God adds to it. The parable of the talents shows us that God gives us even more when we use what He has already given us. Jesus told His disciples, *For whoever has, to him more will be given* (Matt. 13:12). Every time our faith grows, God will give us even more!

Third, God acts sovereignly – completely separate from our faith. He works His eternal purposes not because of our level of faith, but simply because He is God. At those times, the initiative is His, not ours.

Since God is infinitely greater than our ability to understand Him, we can't comprehend all the why's and how's of His mysterious ways. He simply gives us directions, and it is our task is to trust and obey. Again, God sometimes acts sovereignly, apart from our faith, but He wants us to use the faith that we do have. In Hebrews 11:6 we read, *Without faith it is impossible to please Him.*

It is in learning how to believe that we receive God's blessings and the ability to do His will. Sometimes educated men and women find that simple, childlike faith is the most difficult thing to accomplish. God knows when our faith is weak, but He wants us to take the seed of faith we do have and nurture *it*.

What if a mustard seed expected to be fully grown after only one day? What if it worked with all its might for an entire year, yet still wasn't fully grown? What if each day it measured itself and said, "See, I haven't grown even one inch; it would be wrong of me to call myself a mustard plant. I'll never be of any use!" Using our faith opens our hearts to what faith can do. That is why Satan works so hard to keep us from learning. He wants the seed of faith to lie dormant within us, never to grow. But God has planted that seed in us, and He will cause it to grow when we trust in Him.

Jesus knew that a mustard seed requires several years to grow into a mature, productive plant. He could have told us to have faith like a grain of wheat, a grain that produces a mature plant in only one short season. Or He could have compared our faith to a tiny seed hidden in the cone of a cedar of Lebanon, a tree that requires seventy years to reach its towering height. Instead, He spoke of faith as a mustard seed. Jesus doesn't ask unreasonable things of us. What may seem difficult, even impossible at times, becomes possible, even reasonable, with Christ who is the author and finisher of our faith. We can trust that our faith is growing if we give it a chance.

I'm convinced that we can hasten death if we fail to learn more about trusting God. On one occasion fear nearly caused me to meet my Maker. I had always wanted to swim under water without having to surface constantly for air. A friend loaned me his scuba-diving equipment, but he knew nothing about it except how to strap it on. He knew nothing about the dangers involved, so he didn't know enough to tell me how careful I should be. With no fear I plunged into the Atlantic Ocean. Just as I expected, it was exciting and amazing. There I was – swimming with the fish.

Suddenly something happened to the breathing apparatus. There was no oxygen! I had to get to the surface, and quickly! Then it hit me – panic! With overwhelming fear I raced upward. When I hit the surface, I gulped for air and managed to get both air and water into my lungs. Sputtering and coughing, I struggled to divest myself of the air tank so I could stay afloat, but it was more difficult to get off in the water than it had been to put on while on dry land. For seemingly endless minutes I thrashed about desperately, realizing that the tank would soon weigh me down. Terror seemed to wipe out my ability to think clearly.

Needless to say, I survived that ordeal. How, I'm not quite sure, but what a quick, violent lesson I received about the potentially fatal power of fear. Now, as I look back on the experience, I see that my loving Father was merely giving me yet one more free lesson on the importance of living in faith rather than in fear.

Faith does not change God's mind. He already knows what we need. Rather, faith changes the person who is doing the believing. We should pray and believe – we should *keep on* praying and believing – that our faith is growing and that we are being changed into the image of Christ. *Choose* to believe, and watch your faith grow.

One of the most cherished and exciting times of my day is my early morning prayer walk. During this time I practice believing that I'm receiving what God has available for me. I rejoice that my heart and lungs are working better, that my bones are being made stronger, that my entire body is singing with new health through the gifts that Jesus provides me. I believe and rejoice in the knowledge that something good is being accomplished in me.

I practice believing that God is working in my spirit to cleanse me, inspire me, make me a better servant, give me more zeal, and help me to love Him more and to love people more. After a while I feel in my spirit that I'm experiencing the mounting up on wings like an eagle that Isaiah wrote about.

Chapter 19

Maturing in Faith

If our faith remains fragile, we will live in an ambiguous situation of sometimes-believing God and at other times wrestling with doubts and uncertainties. We desperately need to grow in faith in order to be better prepared for the last days just prior to the return of Christ. Those days will be more stressful, more horrible than most of us have ever experienced. Natural disasters such as earthquakes, hurricanes, tornadoes, floods, droughts, famines and plagues will increase in all parts of the world.

We may lose all electrical power and gasoline. Within days – even hours – medical help could be minimal to nonexistent. Sources of food and water could be gone within hours. If the mere thought of losing these things brings fear to your heart, just think of what the actual experience would be like!

Regardless of how well our families or friends are doing, fear can give us a vague but relentless uneasiness that *something* is wrong. Fear that lies hidden in our hearts can make us feel that we must do something more to protect our loved ones from unseen dangers. The Bible tells us that the wise person anticipates trouble and prepares for it (see Prov. 22:3). But God has also told us to trust Him, and never to be anxious over such concerns. Satan, our enemy wants us to fear that some unknown tragedy is always just around the corner. These kinds of fears will gnaw away at our peace of mind unless we learn how to increase our faith.

Peter experienced a phenomenal miracle when he walked on water, but for some reason his fear was stronger than his faith. When he saw the waves, he sank. You and I may be in a state of physical prosperity and emotional stability, with everything going our way. But if we have not learned how to defeat fear, we are not prepared for the future.

The key is to believe that whatever happens is a God-given opportunity for us to trust Him. If Peter had understood that, instead of being afraid he could have shouted, "Hey, Jesus, here comes a big wave! Are we going for a swim?"

Maturing in faith accomplishes three things.

First, it pleases God: *Without faith it is impossible to please Him* (Heb. 11:6). And He is pleased when we believe without requiring physical evidence, as stated in Hebrews 11:1: *Faith is . . . the evidence of things not seen.*

Second, it makes us happier and helps us feel that our lives have accomplished something worthwhile.

Third, it helps us to give blessings to others. Every day I receive hundreds of letters and many telephone calls from people who thank me for helping them to find their way out of difficult problems. My faith journey has helped them, and they in turn encourage me. And I'm inspired even more to seek out those who have not yet learned how to help their faith to mature.

Faith is somewhat like a cup of hot coffee (or your favorite beverage). Picture yourself on a bitter cold evening walking through fierce, freezing winds and then arriving home. Someone hands you a steaming hot cup of your favorite beverage. You eagerly clasp the warm cup and feel its warmth triggering pleasure in your cold hands.

At that point do you have the warm cup? Yes, you have it, but it still is not *in you.*

You can have a kind of faith that you cling to but has not yet made its way *into* your heart. You want to believe, and strive to believe, but confidence eludes you.

Now imagine the difference that you feel when you drink the hot beverage. Now you really have it. It creates a warm glow in you, just as Romans 5:5 reminds you: *The love of God has been poured out in [your heart]*.

Maturing faith creates a warm glow of confidence that God is working through you to accomplish His purpose. This faith abides in you and does not require that you strain to receive its benefits. In fact, the more you strain, the less effective your faith may be!

One illustration stands out in my mind. Mary and I were at a Korean church in New York. When I invited those who wanted to be prayed for to come forward, hundreds moved toward the front of the church. The pastor organized them into a line, and the people waited patiently for Mary and me to pray with each person.

There were so many people wanting prayer that it seemed we prayed for hours. Around 1:00 a.m. the last family stood before us – a man, a woman, and a teenage boy. I was so tired that I didn't ask what they wanted us to pray about. Since we did not know what they wanted, I made a simple prayer for God to meet whatever need they had. But as I prayed, I knew God had met their need. I cannot explain exactly how I knew, but when that confidence comes, I've learned to recognize it.

Later that morning we were scheduled to have breakfast with the pastor. We were surprised to see that same family accompanying him. They did not speak English, but I could tell they were quite excited about something. The pastor explained it to us. They had waited so long to be prayed for because their need was so great. Their teenage son was scheduled for surgery to remove an orange-sized cancer from his knee. When they returned home after our prayer, the son said, "Look at my knee!" The cancer was gone!

Can you imagine how thankful I was that God had given us the privilege of praying for that family? Can you understand why I am so passionately interested in doing whatever I can to help my faith to mature? Do you understand why I am so eager to encourage everyone to do whatever possible to grow in faith?

In closing, I speak to those of you who have never seen or experienced a miracle. You may be tempted to feel like a second-class Christian. Don't!

What is a mighty, powerful faith? You and I may want faith that moves mountains, cures cancer and arthritis, or eliminates pain in a loved one. That kind of faith is needed, but I think God's favorite faith is outlined in Hebrews 11. Those saints had strong enough faith to believe God even though some of them never received in this life what God had promised. Abraham must have been God's favorite example, and he died *before* all of God's promises to him were fulfilled. Abraham refused to doubt. When you and I also refuse to doubt, we become God's future stars.

Practice believing that you are the happiest person in the world, even if your emotions tell you it isn't true. God honors whatever you believe. Go for a walk and believe that every step takes you one step closer to heaven. Practice believing until faith overcomes your doubts. Believe that the righteousness of Christ is His gift to you not because of your goodness, but because of His goodness. Practice believing that every breath you breathe increases your health and joy.

Think, believe, and declare victory in Christ – victory like winning the championship. Victory over every problem and every disease. But what if you die, as we all will eventually? Here is the answer: *Death is swallowed up in victory* (1 Cor. 15:54).

When you step from this life into the next, God will roll out the red carpet. You will have fought the good fight. You will have kept the faith. You will hear Him say:

Well done, good and faithful servant!

About the Author

Merlin R. Carothers' books have been translated into 53 languages. A Master Parachutist in the 82nd Airborne Division during three major campaigns of World War II where he served as a guard to General Dwight D. Eisenhower. Later, as a Lt. Colonel in the U.S. Army Chaplaincy he served in Europe, Korea, the Dominican Republic, Panama and Vietnam. He is a pilot, lecturer and retired pastor. He has made many appearances on national television and has traveled worldwide to share what he has learned.

Merlin and Mary live in San Marcos, California.

Postlude

Mary and I have read every page in this book many times. Each reading has increased our own joy. We encourage you to re-read each page.

If this book has been a blessing to you, please let us know. Every month we prepare *Praise News* in which we share new things that we learn about praise. We will be pleased to send this to you at no charge, on request. You can contact us at:

Merlin R. Carothers
Foundation of Praise
PO Box 2518, Dept. B17
Escondido, CA 92033-2518
Or visit our website at www.merlincarothers.com

VICTORY ON PRAISE MOUNTAIN **$9.00**
Spontaneous praise often leads into valleys that are direct paths to higher ground.

THE BIBLE ON PRAISE **$3.00**
A beautiful front cover painting by Merlin. Features Merlin's favorite selected verses on praise from thirty-eight books of the Bible.

MORE POWER TO YOU **$9.00**
Written for persons in every day places who need more power in their every day lives.

WHAT'S ON YOUR MIND? **$9.00**
Would you be ashamed for everyone you know to see your thoughts? If so, you urgently need to read and understand *What's On Your Mind?*.

LET ME ENTERTAIN YOU **$7.00**
After years of serving the Lord Merlin was eager to retire. He wanted to rest, relax and enjoy a quiet life, but God had other plans for him.

PRAISE CLASSICS **$10.00**
Prison to Praise and *Power in Praise* in a hardcover edition.

YOU CAN BE HAPPY NOW **$9.00**
Everyone desires to be happy! This book will help you to understand how much God wants you to be happy.

Please enclose $4.00 for shipping.

AWARD WINNING MOVIE

A true story based on the book with more than 15 million copies in print!

A First Place award by "National Religious Broadcasters."

An Angel award by "Excellence in Media."

A First Place Covenant Award by "The Southern Baptist Radio and Television Commission."

ISBN 0-943026-33-4

If you didn't believe in miracles before, you will after watching *Prison to Praise*.

A sixty minute DVD that is loved by children and adults.

Available for $16.00 from:
Foundation of Praise
PO Box 2518 Dept. M-B17
Escondido CA 92033-2518

Please enclose $4.00
for shipping on all orders